# 13th International Joint Conference on Natural Language Processing and the 3rd Conference of the Asia-Pacific Chapter of the Association for Computational Linguistics (IJCNLP-AACL 2023)



Tutorial Abstracts

Nusa Dua, Indonesia
1 - 4 November 2023

ISBN: 978-1-7138-9000-3

**Printed from e-media with permission by:**

Curran Associates, Inc.
57 Morehouse Lane
Red Hook, NY 12571

**Some format issues inherent in the e-media version may also appear in this print version.**



Printed with permission by Curran Associates, Inc. (2024)

For permission requests, please contact the Association for Computational Linguistics at the address below.

Association for Computational Linguistics
209 N. Eighth Street
Stroudsburg, Pennsylvania 18360

Phone: 1-570-476-8006
Fax: 1-570-476-0860

acl@aclweb.org

**Additional copies of this publication are available from:**

Curran Associates, Inc.
57 Morehouse Lane
Red Hook, NY 12571 USA
Phone: 845-758-0400
Fax: 845-758-2633
Email: curran@proceedings.com
Web: www.proceedings.com

IJCNLP-AACL 2023

# The 13th International Joint Conference on Natural Language Processing and the 3rd Conference of the Asia-Pacific Chapter of the Association for Computational Linguistics

## Proceedings of the Conference (Tutorial Abstracts)

November 1 – 4, 2023

The IJCNLP-AACL organizers gratefully acknowledge the support from the following sponsors.

**Platinum**

**Gold**

**Silver**

Order copies of this and other ACL proceedings from:

Association for Computational Linguistics (ACL)
209 N. Eighth Street
Stroudsburg, PA 18360
USA
Tel: +1-570-476-8006
Fax: +1-570-476-0860
acl@aclweb.org

# Message from the General Chair

Welcome to IJCNLP-AACL 2023, the 17th International Joint Conference on Natural Language Processsing (IJCNLP) and the 3rd Conference of the Asia-Pacific Chapter of the Association for Computational Linguistics (AACL). The conference will be held in Nusa Dua, Bali, Indonesia, during November 1-4, 2023.

The joint conferences of IJCNLP and AACL are organized by alternating leadership in the Asia-Pacific region, in odd years by Asian Federation of Natural Language Processing (AFNLP) and in even years by AACL, except when the annual meetings of ACL are offered in the region every three years, in which case the conferences will be offered and organized solely by ACL. This year, the conference is organized by AFNLP.

As President of AFNLP, I have formed the Conference Coordination Committee (CCC) last year with executive members of AFNLP: Sadao Kurohashi (Vice President), Min Zhang (Secretary), Liang-Chih Yu (Honorary Treasurer), and Minghui Dong (Web Master). Xuanjing Huang has participated in the meetings of the committee as AACL Representative. I am truly thankful for their dedication in the initial stages as CCC members, in particular during the selection of the Local Chairs together with the conference venue and the nomination and appointment of General Chair and Program Committee Chairs, and, after it is decided that I also serve as General Chair of the conference, for their service as respective chairs throughout the conference preparation stages. Their continued support has been of tremendous help and is much appreciated.

I would also like to thank deeply the entire organizing committee of the conference for their hardwork and superb handling of difficult situations, most of all due to the much limited time to address their respective tasks.

- Program Committe Chairs: Yuki Arase, Baotian Hu and Wei Lu have managed the most critical task of establishing the main program of the conference, which includes, among many others, forming and coordinating the Program Committee, constructing the call for papers with a timely theme track, overseeing the review process on both Softconf and ARR, making decisions on paper acceptance, selecting keynote speakers and putting together the program schedule, and most of all communicating with the reviewers, authors, and other committee members over numerous times during the entire process. This is a formidable task, and their efforts for leading to its successful completion are so much appreciated.

- Tutorial Chairs: Yun-Nung (Vivian) Chen and Sadao Kurohashi have gone through the tutorial proposals to select six tutorials that are well balanced both topically and geographically, actively fostering diversity and inclusion.

- Workshop Chairs: Kehai Chen and Lun-Wei Ku have gone over the workshop proposals to select eight strong workshops, NLPMC, WIESP, Eval4NLP, SocialNLP, SEA, FinNLP, NLInt, and ArtOfSafety.

- Demo Chairs: Sriparna Saha and Herry Sujaini have overseen the process of selecting papers among those submitted to the system demonstration session independently of the main program.

- Publication Chairs: Minghui Dong and Kotaro Funakoshi have put together all the documents and articles to construct the conference proceedings expertly, cordially and in a timely manner.

- Sponsorship Chairs: Min Zhang, Satoshi Sekine, Haofeng Wang, and Zhongqing Wang have worked hard to solicit funding to support the conference, and successfully, despite the short time to operate. We are all much grateful to the funding organizations for their generous help.

- Finance Chair: Liang-Chih Yu has always been the person to consult whenever any financial issues arise. Things are not yet fully over at the time of preparing for this message, but are believed to come to self-sustainment, with some room for financial aid as well, thanks to the valiant efforts of all the people involved.
- Website & App Chair: Juntao Li has worked single-handedly and dependably to reflect all the requests to post important news at our conference homepage.
- Publicity & Social Media Chairs: Koustava Goswami and JinYeong Bak have worked to disseminate information over social media as widely as possible whenever there are notable events for the conference.
- Handbook Chairs: Yasuhide Miura and Yunita Sari have worked very hard to meet the deadline for the conference handbook when there is really not much time left. The help of Sonoko Miura as Conference Handbook Designer is also gratefully acknowledged.
- Faculty Advisors to Student Research Workshop (SRW): Hyeju Jang, Yugo Murawaki, and Derek Fai Wong have worked to oversee the SRW, in particular communicating with its chairs, Dongfang Li, Rahmad Mahendra and Zilu Peter Tang. The efforts of the faculty advisors and SRW chairs are much appreciated.
- Diversity & Inclusion Chair: Hwanhee Lee has worked to resolve requests for financial aid, mostly in the form of registration waiver, and as amicably as possible, under a strict limit on granting such requests.
- Registration Chair: Dessi Puji Lestari has worked to oversee the process of registration, together with the kind help of Minghui Dong as the manager of the registration site.
- Local Chairs: Derry Wijaya, Ayu Purwarianti and Adila Alfa Krisnadhi have worked to resolve practically numerous issues, many times beyond the duties of local chairs, after successfully bidding to host the conference in Nusa Dua, Bali, Indonesia. It is with much gratitude and respect that I commend their efforts to the fullest.

In summary, I can only say that their sense of duty and responsibility has been critical to meeting and resolving so many difficulties that we faced along the way. Many, many thanks to all of them.

The mode of the conference has been determined early on to be hybrid, considering the fact that we are not fully over the coronavirus pandemic. However, it has not been quite clear until very recently whether we would need, and can afford, the top-notch professional service of an on-demand video platform such as Underline for a hybrid conference. I am very grateful to all the chairs for the remarkable patience and very happy with the concerted decision to go for the service of Underline, albeit in a limited scope. I wish to thank kindly Damira Mrsic and Sol Rosenberg, representatives of Underline, for the patience and expert help. I also thank Richard Gerber for the help with our use of Softconf.

The Local Chairs made a proposal to host the conference in Nusa Dua early on, but it took all of us a long time to finally come to a decision to choose Grand Hyatt Bali, Nusa Dua, Bali, Indonesia for its exceptional location in the region as the conference venue. Its daytime temperatures are expected to reach 31°C, with the nighttime temperatures of around 24°C. I wish a very pleasant time for all the off-line participants of the conference and an equally memorable time for all the on-line participants.

Welcome to the conference and Nusa Dua!

IJCNLP-AACL 2023 General Chair
Jong C. Park
Korea Advanced Institute of Science and Technology (KAIST)

# Message from the Program Committee Co-Chairs

Welcome to IJCNLP-AACL 2023, the 13th International Joint Conference on Natural Language Processing and the 3rd Conference of the Asia-Pacific Chapter of the Association for Computational Linguistics. This year, we have organized the conference in a hybrid format to accommodate both in-person and virtual participation, making it accessible to everyone regardless of travel constraints. The physical conference takes place in Bali; we are looking forward to discussions on present and future research in NLP with all of you.

This conference has been made possible through the dedicated voluntary efforts of hundreds of individuals. We sincerely thank everyone involved, in particular:

- The incredible team of 30 SACs, 72 ACs, and 427 reviewers who carefully handled submissions.
- Our Best Paper Award Committee, Danushka Bollegala, Jing Jiang, Yang Liu (Tsinghua University), Nanyun (Violet) Peng, Xiaojun Wan, Taro Watanabe, and Koichiro Yoshino, who assessed the candidate papers under the tight schedule.
- Computational Linguistics Editor-in-Chief, Hwee Tou Ng, for exploring the presentation possibility of CL papers with us.
- The ARR technical team, Jonathan Kummerfeld, Nils Dycke, Yoshitomo Matsubara, Dhruv Naik, and Amanda Stent, for supporting IJCNLP-AACL 2023 to have submissions through ARR.
- Rich Gerber at Softconf, who always addressed our inquiries and issues quickly.
- The Program Chairs of conferences going on the same period of time, including Houda Bouamor, Juan Pino, Kalika Bali (EMNLP 2023), Maria Keet, Hung-Yi Lee, Sina Zarrieß (INLG 2023), Svetlana Stoyanchev, Shafiq Joty (SIGDIAL 2023), and Jennifer Dy, Sriraam Natarajan, Kristian Kersting, Sameer Singh, Prasad Tadepalli, Angela Yao (AAAI 2024), whom we cooperated with to preclude multiple submissions.
- The ACL Executive Committee, especially Yusuke Miyao (Conference Officer), for supporting IJCNLP-AACL 2023 with various advice on conference organization.
- The ACL Ethics Committee, Min-Yen Kan, for advising us to conduct ethics reviews.
- The past *ACL conference program chairs, in particular Jordan Boyd-Graber, Naoaki Okazaki, Anna Rogers (ACL 2023) for sharing their experiences that were crucial to avoid pitfalls and practically sharing tools to handle a large volume of submissions.
- ACL Anthology director, Matt Post, for supporting us to publish the proceedings.
- Underline team, Jernej Masnec, Luka Simic, Sol Rosenberg, Borna Bevanda, and Damira Mrsic (Underline Science, Inc.), for their professional services and supports to realize the online part of the conference.

The conference owes its existence to the collaborative efforts of multiple chairs of IJCNLP-AACL 2023. We are deeply grateful to:

- General Chair, Jong C. Park, who was responsible for and led the whole process.
- Publication Chairs, Minghui Dong and Kotaro Funakoshi, for compiling the proceedings and ensuring the correct formatting.

- Handbook Chairs, Yunita Sari and Yasuhide Miura, for creating the conference handbooks.
- Web Chair, Juntao Li, and Publicity & Social Media chairs, JinYeong Bak and Koustava Goswami, for distributing the important information on the web, which allowed efficient and timely communication.
- Local Chairs, Derry Wijaya, Ayu Purwarianti, and Adila Alfa Krisnadhi, who did everything for realizing the physical part of the conference.
- Our assistants, Jindi Yu, Senbao Shi, and Jiaxi Li for their help and support throughout the conference preparation period.

Last but not least, we extend our heartfelt gratitude to all the authors for their invaluable scientific contributions, which are at the very heart of IJCNLP-AACL 2023. We hope everyone will enjoy IJCNLP-AACL 2023 either on-site or online.

## Submission and Acceptance

IJCNLP-AACL 2023 used two submission platforms: direct submission through SoftConf and submissions through ACL Rolling Review (ARR). We received 338 direct submissions (229 long and 109 short) and 25 commitments from ARR (19 long and 6 short), in total 363 valid papers went through the review process. The submissions came from 33 countries and regions of all over the world: 49.2% from Asia-Pacific, 26.7% from North America, 18.7% from Europe, 4.1% from Middle East, and 1.3% from Africa.

The direct submissions were thoroughly reviewed by 427 reviewers under 72 ACs and 30 SACs in 19 tracks. The ARR committed papers were handled by the SACs based on review and meta-review comments gained through ARR. Finally, we have accepted 94 submissions (72 long and 22 short) as the main conference papers accompanied by 37 Findings papers (23 long and 14 short), which results in the acceptance rates of 25.9% for the main conference (29.0% long and 19.1% short) and 36.1% when including the Findings papers (38.3% long and 31.3% short).

In adherence to the ACL code of ethics, we have conducted ethics reviews. Given the limited number of papers that raised ethical concerns, the program chairs assumed the responsibilities of ethics reviewers. Authors of papers that received ethics review comments were requested to address these concerns in their final versions.

The papers accepted to the main conference will be presented in the form of either oral and poster presentations. The presentation modes were determined solely based on the nature of the work, irrespective of review scores. There is no distinction in the proceedings regarding the presentation modes. The Findings papers will have optional lightning talks to introduce highlights of their work.

## Design of Tracks

IJCNLP-AACL 2023 has incorporated 18 general areas reflecting the trends of the field. Most of these areas are consistent with the recent $*$ACL conferences. In addition, recognizing the conference centers on Asia-Pacific regions, which boast a variety of regional languages with limited language resources, we have introduced a special theme track this year: Large Language Models and Regional/Low-Resource Languages. The most popular areas were "NLP Applications," "Resources and Evaluation," and "Large Language Models and Regional/Low-Resource Languages."

- Dialogue and Interactive Systems
- Discourse and Pragmatics

- Generation and Summarization
- Information Extraction
- Information Retrieval and Text Mining
- Interpretability and Analysis of Models for NLP
- Language Modeling and Analysis
- Linguistic Theories, Cognitive Modeling, and Psycholinguistics
- Machine Learning for NLP
- Machine Translation and Multilingualism
- Multimodality: Speech, Vision, Robotics, and Beyond
- NLP Applications
- Question Answering
- Resources and Evaluation
- Semantics: Lexical, Sentence-level Semantics, Textual Inference, etc.
- Sentiment Analysis, Stylistic Analysis, and Argument Mining
- Society and NLP
- Syntax: Tagging, Chunking, Parsing, etc.
- Theme Track: Large Language Models and Regional/Low-Resource Languages

## Limitations Section and Responsible NLP Checklist

Following ACL 2023, EMNLP 2022, and ARR, we made it mandatory to discuss limitations of a study and submit the responsible NLP checklist to foster the open and honest scientific discussions and promote consideration of responsibility in NLP research. We also encouraged authors to include Ethics Statements whenever there might be potential concerns. The Limitations Section and Ethics Statements did not count towards the page limit.

## Best Paper Awards

Following the new ACL conference awards policy, we organized the Best Paper Award Committee to select the Best Paper Awards followed by Outstanding Paper Awards, together with two special awards, namely Social Impact Award and Resource Award. The committee assessed 15 papers nominated by reviewers. In addition, SACs of each track selected at most a paper for Area Chair's Awards. The award winners will be announced in a dedicated plenary session on November 4, 2023.

IJCNLP-AACL 2023 Program Comittee Co-Chairs
Yuki Arase (Osaka University)
Baotian Hu (Harbin Institute of Technology (Shenzhen))
Wei Lu (Singapore University of Technology and Design)

# Message from the Local Co-Chairs

It is with immense excitement and a profound sense of achievement that we, the local co-chairs of IJCNLP-AACL 2023 - Ayu Purwarianti, Adila Krisnadhi, and myself - welcome you to the breathtaking island of Bali, Indonesia. The significance of this moment cannot be understated, as it marks the very first time that the IJCNLP or ACL conference has found its home in the enchanting Indonesian archipelago. This landmark occasion has doubled our excitement as local chairs, and we are thrilled to share this unique experience with all of you.

Since the moment when we were awarded the privilege of organizing IJCNLP-AACL 2023, we have been tirelessly working to ensure this conference exceeds all expectations. We embarked on an extensive quest to discover the perfect venue and event organizer, negotiated hybrid support, searched for sponsorships, all while meticulously managing the budget, and addressing an array of logistical details, all with the goal of enhancing your experience at the conference. While our commitment to delivering an exceptional event has remained steadfast, we did encounter some noteworthy challenges. The close proximity of EMNLP 2023, scheduled in nearby Singapore just one month after IJCNLP-AACL 2023 and whose submission deadline is also just a month after IJCNLP-AACL 2023's, might have created scheduling dilemmas for prospective authors and participants. We sincerely hope that, despite these challenges, our captivating Bali location will draw participants from around the globe, ensuring IJCNLP-AACL 2023 remains a highlight in the NLP conference calendar.

Another notable challenge has been attracting local participants to the conference. The absence of Scopus indexing for IJCNLP or AACL proceedings, a critical factor for researchers in Indonesia, has presented hurdles. We hope that in the future, as more NLP proceedings are indexed by Scopus, we can generate greater local interest and participation in the region.

On behalf of the local organizing team, I extend my heartfelt gratitude and appreciation to our General Chair, Jong Park; Publication Co-Chair, Minghui Dong; Finance Chair, Liang-Chih Yu; Tutorial Co-Chair, Sadao Kurohashi; Sponsorship Chair, Min Zhang; Registration Chair, Dessi Puji Lestari; and the PC co-chairs who have given so much help and support to the local co-chairs. I have learned a lot from you. Hosting the AACL-IJCNLP 2023 has been an invaluable learning experience for me, and it is an experience I will carry with me. I am also grateful for the contributions and hard work of the entire organizing committee and our kind sponsors, without whom none of this would have been possible.

We look forward to the exciting discussions, sharing of knowledge, and camaraderie that will define IJCNLP-AACL 2023. Welcome to Bali, and we sincerely hope you have one of the most wonderful conference experiences.

Warm regards,

IJCNLP-AACL 2023 Local Co-Chairs
Derry Tanti Wijaya (Monash University Indonesia)
Ayu Purwarianti (Institut Teknologi Bandung)
Adila Krisnadhi (Universitas Indonesia)

# Organizing Committee

## General Chair

Jong C. Park, Korea Advanced Institute of Science and Technology (KAIST)

## Program Committee Chairs

Yuki Arase, Osaka University
Baotian Hu, Harbin Insitute of Technology (Shenzhen)
Wei Lu, Singapore University of Technology and Design

## Tutorial Chairs

Yun-Nung (Vivian) Chen, National Taiwan University
Sadao Kurohashi, Kyoto University

## Workshop Chairs

Kehai Chen, Harbin Institute of Technology (Shenzhen)
Lun-Wei Ku, Academia Sinica

## Demo Chairs

Sriparna Saha, Indian Institute of Technology (Patna)
Herry Sujaini, University of Tanjunpura

## Publication Chairs

Minghui Dong, Institute for Infocomm Research, A*Star
Kotaro Funakoshi, Tokyo Institute of Technology

## Sponsorship Chairs

Min Zhang, Harbin Institute of Technology (Shenzhen)
Satoshi Sekine, RIKEN, AIP
Haofeng Wang, Tongji University (Shanghai)
Zhongqing Wang, Soochow University

## Finance Chair

Liang-Chih Yu, Yuan Ze University

## Website & App Chair

Juntao Li, Soochow University

## Publicity & Social Media Chairs

Koustava Goswami, Adobe Research India
JinYeong Bak, SungKyunKwan University

**Handbook Chairs**

Yasuhide Miura, Fujifilm Corporation
Yunita Sari, Universitas Gadjah Mada
(Conference Handbook Designer: Sonoko Miura)

**Faculty Advisors to Student Research Workshop**

Hyeju Jang, Indiana University-Purdue University Indianapolis
Yugo Murawaki, Kyoto University
Derek Fai Wong, University of Macau

**Diversity & Inclusion Chair**

Hwanhee Lee, Chung Ang University

**Registration Chair**

Dessi Puji Lestari, Bandung Institute of Technology

**Local Chairs**

Derry Wijaya, Monash University Indonesia
Ayu Purwarianti, Bandung Institute of Technology
Adila Alfa Krisnadhi, University of Indonesia

**AACL Representative**

Xuanjing Huang, Fudan University

# Program Comittee

**Dialogue and Interactive Systems**

Senior area chair: Michel Galley
Area chairs: Song Feng, Alexandros Papangelis, Lei Sha, Wei-Nan Zhang

**Discourse and Pragmatics**

Senior area chair: Bonnie Webber
Area chair: Yufang Hou

**Generation and Summarization**

Senior area chairs: Yue Dong, Dimitra Gkatzia
Area chairs: Meng Cao, Khyathi Raghavi Chandu, Bang Liu, Saad Mahamood, Lili Mou, Arabella Sinclair, Wen Xiao, Jiacheng Xu

**Information Extraction**

Senior area chairs: Ruihong Huang, Makoto Miwa
Area chairs: Jun Araki, Prafulla Kumar Choubey, Fenia Christopoulou, Wenlin Yao

**Information Retrieval and Text Mining**

Senior area chairs: Sophia Ananiadou, Muhao Chen
Area chairs: Yixin Cao, Fangyu Liu, Tulika Saha, Sheng Zhang, Hongming Zhang

**Interpretability and Analysis of Models for NLP**

Senior area chair: Kai-Wei Chang
Area chairs: Sunipa Dev, Yangfeng Ji, Xiaoqing Zheng

**Language Modeling and Analysis**

Senior area chairs: Naoya Inoue, Yang Liu (Microsoft)
Area chairs: Benjamin Heinzerling, Reid Pryzant, Keisuke Sakaguchi, Rui Zhang

**Linguistic Theories, Cognitive Modeling, and Psycholinguistics**

Senior area chairs: Ashutosh Modi, Yohei Oseki
Area chair: Pranava Madhyastha

**Machine Learning for NLP**

Senior area chairs: Lingpeng Kong, Sinno Jialin Pan
Area chairs: Jing Ma, Zhiyong Wu, Jingjing Xu, Shi Zong

**Machine Translation and Multilingualism**

Senior area chairs: Longyue Wang, Deyi Xiong
Area chairs: Liangyou Li, Xing Niu, Elena Voita, Baosong Yang, Biao Zhang

**Multimodality: Speech, Vision, Robotics, and Beyond**

Senior area chairs: Li Dong, Sakriani Sakti
Area chairs: Armen Aghajanyan, Zhe Gan, Florian Metze

**NLP Applications**

Senior area chairs: Jey Han Lau, Mingxuan Wang
Area chairs: Shanbo Cheng, Massimo Piccardi, Ehsan Shareghi, Yangqiu Song, Ekaterina Vylomova, Rong Ye, Zhirui Zhang

**Question Answering**

Senior area chair: Wenpeng Yin
Area chairs: Nitish Gupta, Hangfeng He, Zhiguo Wang

**Resources and Evaluation**

Senior area chairs: Eduardo Blanco, Joel Tetreault
Area chairs: Yvette Graham, Anne Lauscher, Junyi Jessy Li, Liling Tan, Alakananda Vempala

**Semantics: Lexical, Sentence-level Semantics, Textual Inference, etc.**

Senior area chair: Preslav Nakov
Area chairs: Atsushi Fujita, James Thorne, Marcos Zampieri

**Sentiment Analysis, Stylistic Analysis, and Argument Mining**

Senior area chair: Vincent Ng
Area chairs: Henning Wachsmuth, Jianfei Yu

**Society and NLP**

Senior area chair: Wei Gao
Area chairs: Firoj Alam, Shi Feng, Kokil Jaidka, Liang-Chih Yu

**Syntax: Tagging, Chunking, Parsing etc.**

Senior area chair: Kewei Tu
Area chair: Zhenghua Li

**Theme Track: Large Language Models and Regional/Low-Resource Languages**

Senior area chairs: Lei Li, Imed Zitouni
Area chairs: Boxing Chen, Zhiyu Chen, Stephan Peitz, Zhaopeng Tu, Lina Yao

**Reviewers**

Asad Abdi, Haithem Afli, Piush Aggarwal, Akiko Aizawa, Md. Shad Akhtar, Hend Al-Khalifa, Bharat Ram Ambati, Jie An, Anietie Andy, Eiji ARAMAKI, Arturo Argueta, Piyush Arora, Lukasz Augustyniak

Xuefeng Bai, Amir Bakarov, Mithun Balakrishna, Timothy Baldwin, Hritik Bansal, Christine Basta, Gábor Berend, Sabine Bergler, Dario Bertero, Arnab Bhattacharya, Pushpak Bhattacharyya, Anahita Bhiwandiwalla, Michael Bloodgood, Victoria Bobicev, Florian Boudin, Thomas Brovelli (Meyer), Wray Buntine, Miriam Butt

John Calvo Martinez, Ziqiang Cao, Spencer Caplan, Rémi Cardon, Dumitru-Clementin Cercel, Tuhin Chakrabarty, Tanmoy Chakraborty, Yllias Chali, Hou Pong Chan, Kehai Chen, Yubo Chen, Mei-Hua Chen, Xiaocong Chen, Yue Chen, Hsin-Hsi Chen, Fuxiang Chen, Hannah Chen, Sihao Chen, Xinchi Chen, Qian Chen, Qiang Chen, Kanzhi Cheng, Colin Cherry, Emmanuele Chersoni, KEY-SUN CHOI, Monojit Choudhury, Chenhui Chu, Abu Nowshed Chy

Aswarth Abhilash Dara, Avisha Das, Sarthak Dash, Gael de Chalendar, Mathieu Dehouck, Vera Demberg, Yue Deng, Yuntian Deng, Shumin Deng, Chris Develder, Maria Pia di Buono, Luigi Di Caro, Gaël Dias, Miguel Domingo, Shichao Dong, Mingwen Dong, Zi-Yi Dou, Aleksandr Drozd, Wanyu Du, Cunxiao Du, Junwen Duan, Kevin Duh, Jonathan Dunn

Hiroshi Echizen'ya, Steffen Eger, Ramy Eskander

Ming Fang, Hao Fei, Elisabetta Fersini, Alejandro Figueroa, Mauajama Firdaus, Margaret Fleck

Matteo Gabburo, Olivier Galibert, Abbas Ghaddar, Pranav Goel, Carlos Gómez-Rodríguez, Jesús González-Rubio, Isao Goto, Yulia Grishina, Yi Guan, Anupam Guha, Tunga Gungor

Udo Hahn, Na-Rae Han, Ting Han, Jie Hao, Maram Hasanain, Sabit Hassan, Yoshihiko Hayashi, Jie He, DELIA IRAZU HERNANDEZ FARIAS, Tsutomu Hirao, Tosho Hirasawa, Yi-Li Hsu, Po Hu, han hu, zhiyuan hu, Hang Hua, Shujian Huang, Zhongqiang Huang, Kaiyu Huang, Hen-Hsen Huang, Tenghao Huang, Jiangping Huang, Patrick Huber, Jena D. Hwang

Dmitry Ilvovsky, Kenji Imamura, Takashi Inui, Hitoshi Isahara, Etsuko Ishii, Hayate Iso

Palak Jain, Shoaib Jameel, Abhik Jana, Inigo Jauregi Unanue, Yangfeng Ji, Yuxiang Jia, Ridong Jiang, Jyun-Yu Jiang, Aditya Joshi, Prathyusha Jwalapuram

Besim Kabashi, Lis Kanashiro Pereira, Diptesh Kanojia, Sarvnaz Karimi, Börje Karlsson, Marzena Karpinska, Anisia Katinskaia, Daisuke Kawahara, Casey Kennington, Salam Khalifa, Joo-Kyung Kim, Hwichan Kim, David King, Tracy Holloway King, Julien Kloetzer, Philipp Koehn, Mamoru Komachi, Kanako Komiya, Myoung-Wan Koo, Yannis Korkontzelos, Fajri Koto, Canasai Kruengkrai, Lun-Wei Ku, Roland Kuhn, Shankar Kumar

Matthieu Labeau, Albert Y.S. Lam, Stefan Larson, Hung Le, Lung-Hao Lee, Gurpreet Lehal, Alessandro Lenci, Yves Lepage, Piji Li, Yun Li, Sheng Li, Junyi Li, Alexander Hanbo Li, Jiaqi Li, Bangzheng Li, Dongfang Li, Dingcheng Li, Yanran Li, Yuan-Fang Li, Tao Li, Zuchao Li, Weikang Li, Fangtao Li, Wei Li, Peifeng Li, Zekun Li, Lu Li, Baoli LI, Junhui Li, Si Li, Haoran LI, Chao-Chun Liang, Mark Liberman, Gilbert Lim, Marina Litvak, Fenglin Liu, Yongbin Liu, Qun Liu, Yiqun Liu, Yang Janet Liu, Yue Liu, Yao Liu, Zhe Liu, Han Liu, Sharid Loáiciga, Robert L Logan IV, Quanyu Long, Yunfei Long, Di Lu, Hanjia Lyu

Jianqiang Ma, Mounica Maddela, Tarek Mahmoud, Peter Makarov, Valentin Malykh, Muhammad Arslan Manzoor, Bruno Martins, Sahisnu Mazumder, John P. McCrae, Bridget McInnes, Fanchao Meng, Rui Meng, Tao Meng, Zaiqiao Meng, Mohsen Mesgar, Margot Mieskes, SeyedAbolghasem Mirroshandel,

Abhijit Mishra, Yusuke Miyao, Aditya Mogadala, Diego Molla, Sneha Mondal, Manuel Montes, Lori Moon, Hajime Morita, Larry Moss, Pramod Kaushik Mudrakarta, Emir Munoz, Dragos Munteanu

Masaaki Nagata, Tetsuji Nakagawa, Preksha Nema, Nam Nguyen, Nhung Nguyen, Truc-Vien T. Nguyen, Thien Nguyen, Eric Nichols, Garrett Nicolai, Massimo Nicosia, Jian-Yun Nie, Takashi Ninomiya, Masaaki Nishino, Sergiu Nisioi, Joakim Nivre, Pierre Nugues

Atul Kr. Ojha, Antoni Oliver

Santanu Pal, Chester Palen-Michel, Yi-Cheng Pan, Zhufeng Pan, Liang Pang, Nikos Papasarantopoulos, Jacob Parnell, Ioannis Partalas, Prasanna Parthasarathi, Marius Pasca, Sapan Patel, Pavel Pecina, Hengzhi Pei, Flammie Pirinen, Andrei Popescu-Belis, Fred Popowich, Animesh Prasad, Daniel Preotiuc-Pietro, Laurent Prévot, Emily Prud'hommeaux

Xinying Qiu

Alexandre Rademaker, Surangika Ranathunga, Yanghui Rao, Farzana Rashid, Hanumant Redkar, German Rigau, Anthony Rios, Bryan Routledge, Alla Rozovskaya

Fatiha Sadat, Saurav Sahay, Elizabeth Salesky, Avneesh Saluja, German Sanchis-Trilles, Bishal Santra, Anoop Sarkar, Ryohei Sasano, Asad Sayeed, Shigehiko Schamoni, Stephanie Schoch, William Schuler, Ethan Selfridge, Nasredine Semmar, Gregory Senay, Cory Shain, Raksha Sharma, Artem Shelmanov, Yangyang Shi, Tomohide Shibata, Kai Shu, Maryam Siahbani, Carina Silberer, Diego Silva, Michel Simard, Patrick Simianer, Sunayana Sitaram, Amy Siu, Hyun-Je Song, Xingyi Song, Marlo Souza, Balaji Vasan Srinivasan, Felix Stahlberg, Mark Steedman, Kristina Striegnitz, Yixuan Su, Katsuhito Sudoh, Yoshi Suhara, Derwin Suhartono, Alane Suhr, Kai Sun, Chengjie Sun, Marek Suppa

Zeerak Talat, George Tambouratzis, Akihiro Tamura, Bowen Tan, Zhiyang Teng, Camilo Thorne, Yufei Tian, Nasim Tohidi, Takenobu Tokunaga, Marc Tomlinson, Marwan Torki, Samia Touileb, Aashka Trivedi, Chen-Tse Tsai

Kiyotaka Uchimoto, Masao Utiyama

Rob van der Goot, David Vandyke, Natalia Vanetik, Clara Vania, Shikhar Vashishth, Rakesh Verma, Martin Villalba

Xintong Wang, Wei Wang, Di Wang, Hecong Wang, Zhaowei Wang, Guangtao Wang, Zijie Wang, Dexin Wang, Hai Wang, Wenya Wang, Jianzong Wang, Weiyue Wang, Zhongqing Wang, Hsin-Min Wang, Qingyun Wang, Derry Tanti Wijaya, Gijs Wijnholds, Kam-Fai Wong, Xianchao Wu, Stephen Wu, Fangzhao Wu, Zhiyong Wu

Tong Xiao, Jun Xie, Canwen Xu, Qiongkai Xu, Fangzhi Xu, Ruifeng Xu, Wenduan Xu, Hongfei Xu

Yadollah Yaghoobzadeh, Zhaohui Yan, Muqiao Yang, Eugene Yang, Haiqin Yang, Yaqin Yang, Wei Yang, Tae Yano, Kaisheng Yao, Seid Muhie Yimam, Qingyu Yin, Seunghyun Yoon, Masaharu Yoshioka, Heng Yu, Jianfei Yu, Xinchen Yu, Dong Yu, Frances Yung

Fadi Zaraket, Zenan Zhai, Yuqi Zhang, Zhuosheng Zhang, Tianyi Zhang, Wen Zhang, Dongyan Zhao, Xinran Zhao, Chao Zhao, Boyuan Zheng, Houquan Zhou, Yichao Zhou, Guangyou Zhou, Yi Zhu, Wanzheng Zhu, Su Zhu, Bowei Zou, Vilém Zouhar, Arkaitz Zubiaga

# Outstanding Services

## Outstanding ACs

We are indebt to these area chairs who offered a distinguished and professional meta-reviewing.

Jun Araki, Prafulla Kumar Choubey, Fenia Christopoulou, Shi Feng, Kokil Jaidka, Zhenghua Li, Massimo Piccardi, Lei Sha, Elena Voita, Henning Wachsmuth, Wenlin Yao, Rui Zhang

## Outstanding Reviewers

The community has greatly benefited from these outstanding reviewers who delivered particularly insightful and constructive review comments.

Dario Bertero, Hsin-Hsi Chen, Colin Cherry, Sarthak Dash, Tunga Gungor, Hwichan Kim, Zuchao Li, Tao Li, Han Liu, Sergiu Nisioi, Zhufeng Pan, Anoop Sarkar, Akihiro Tamura, Stephen Wu, Frances Yung

# Table of Contents

# Language and Robotics: Toward Building Robots Coexisting with Human Society Using Language Interface

**Yutaka Nakamura**[1], **Shuhei Kurita**[2], **and Koichiro Yoshino**[1]
[1] Guardian Robot Project (GRP), R-IH, RIKEN, Japan
[2] Center for Advanced Intelligence Project (AIP), RIKEN, Japan
{yutaka.nakamura, shuhei.kurita, koichiro.yoshino}@riken.jp

## 1 Introduction

Robots are one of the archetypes of AI systems we imagine, and the realization of such robots operating in the real world with language interfaces has long been a dream of us. This vision we have dreamed of is rapidly becoming a reality with the contribution of recent advancements in large language models (LLMs). However, there are still many problems that the research community needs to tackle in order for LLMs and other NLP tools to work in the real world.

This introductory tutorial aims to help researchers who will start language and robotics (*LangRobo*) research in the future by summarizing three points: awareness of the community's issues, recent approaches for these issues, and remaining problems. This tutorial requires only basic NLP knowledge: language modeling and basic NLP task definition. We arrange this tutorial involving not only NLP researchers but also robotics researchers in order to raise issues that are relevant to actual robotics problems.

The connection between NLP and robotics is a challenge that has been tackled in the field of robotics for many years; we have faced the difficulties of the problem many times. There are several difficulties in connecting NLP and robotics, but the following three are particularly problematic:

1. The great difference in granularity between language and robot behavior

2. Robotics tasks involving real-world control often do not allow for language ambiguity

3. Language expressions themselves are often ambiguous and require background knowledge or commonsense reasoning to understand them correctly

While the language expressions used for robots are only a few dozen words at most, robots have countless events to consider, such as their motion trajectories and interactions with things in the real world. In other words, in the field of robotics, there are countless events to be considered outside the language framework, and it is impossible to consider all of them in the model. Another important point to consider is the ambiguity of language expressions. Humans often make omissions when utilizing language, and in practice, such omissions are often very important in actual robot tasks. The omission is closely related to multimodal information obtained from the interaction, such as eye gaze and motions. It is nearly impossible to address these issues with NLP alone or robotics alone.

Many recent works have suggested that deep learning or LLMs can provide solutions to these problems. This tutorial summarizes the recent approaches to the language and robotics problem using such learning-based approaches. The goal of this tutorial is to share the discussion on how these problems can be solved in the future.

## 2 Tutorial Content

As the tutorial contents, a researcher who has been working in robotics for a long time will first introduce classic language utilization problems in their field. He also explains how these problems have been solved in recent years by deep learning and LLMs. In the second part, a researcher who has been working in the fields of language and image processing will explain the recent research on coreference and grounding problems in the real world. It is also mentioned that the recent advancement of vision and language research. In the last lecture part, a researcher who has been working in the human-robot interaction research field, including dialogues, will discuss the collaboration between users and robots and the issues of language understanding and situation understanding necessary for such collaboration. Finally, many



*Proceedings of the 13th International Joint Conference on Natural Language Processing and the 3rd Conference of the Asia-Pacific Chapter of the Association for Computational Linguistics (Tutorial Abstracts)*, pages 1–7
November 1–4, 2023. 

unresolved robot problems will be touched upon, and future language and robotics research directions will be discussed.

### 2.1 Language Use in Robotics Field (Nakamura)

In the research field of robotics, navigation and manipulation have been major issues. They used numerical representations (e.g., coordinates and joint angles that indicate the robot's position) as the main focus. On the other hand, logical planning frameworks have been widely applied to robotics, such as STanford Research Institute Problem Solver (STRIPS) (Fikes and Nilsson, 1971) and Planning Domain Definition Language (PDDL) (Fox and Long, 2003). They have been proposed as frameworks for planning in a virtual space, mainly in the block world, using a programing language-like description. Due to the advancement of deep learning since the 2010s, a system was built in 2018 to interpret human instructions given in natural language to perform picking tasks (Hatori et al., 2018). The advancement of large language models (LLMs) is leading several frameworks for interpreting natural languages such as GaTo (Reed et al.), Say Can (Brohan et al., 2023), and RT-1 (Brohan et al., 2022). In addition, research on generative models of human motion, such as the human motion diffusion model (Tevet et al., 2022), is developing, which is expected to enable robots to cooperate with humans in unstructured environments. In this tutorial, we will give an overview of these studies.

### 2.2 Language Understandings in the Real-world (Kurita)

Recent remarkable advancements in natural language processing have enabled a comprehensive understanding of texts in the context of syntactic and semantic analyses, question-answering, summarization, translation, and even dialogue tasks. However, such models often face challenges when dealing with multimodal contexts in the real world. In this tutorial, we explain how current models struggle to handle real-world contexts and provide an overview of language grounding technologies from four perspectives.

The first perspective focuses on vision and language tasks with a single image. Examples of such tasks include image captioning on MS-COCO (Bernardi et al., 2016) and visual question answering (Antol et al., 2015). We discuss the strengths and limitations of these existing tasks, particularly their reliance on limited contextual information from images. We further introduce the referring expression comprehension or simply "visual grounding" task (Kazemzadeh et al., 2014; Plummer et al., 2015; Yu et al., 2016; Mao et al., 2016), which specifies the target object from a referred expression and the relation to the open-vocabulary object detection task.

The second perspective is obtained through videos. We concentrate on the first-person videos here as they are obtained through the motion of the camera wearer. Recently, a large-scale first-person perspective video dataset of Ego4D was proposed (Grauman et al., 2022). This can be extended for robots that navigate in scenes and related language tasks. Although the model learning from videos enriches the model perspectives in the real-world, image frames in videos are constrained to the preset viewpoints when they are recorded.

The third perspective involves 3D scenes and virtual worlds that provide rich contextual information about the captured scenes. Unlike the previous perspectives, this perspective allows the "embodied" experience for the agents in the environments. Examples of such enriched scenes have been proposed, such as ScanNet (Dai et al., 2017) and Matterport 3D (Chang et al., 2017). 3D referring expression comprehension (Chen et al., 2020) and 3D-QA (Azuma et al., 2022) are also interesting spatial understanding with language expressions. These environments also enable visually-grounded interactive textual understanding tasks. One example is vision and language navigation (VLN) (Anderson et al., 2018), where an agent navigates in environments based on visual and textual information. An interesting approach for VLN is a captioning model from navigation paths. Fried et al. (2018) introduced the speaker-model for generating captions for the paths the agent navigates in environments. Several studies used this speaker model for the training dataset augmentation (Tan et al., 2019; Hao et al., 2020). Kurita and Cho (2021) used the speaker model for ranking the possible action candidates during navigation. Recently, Habitat simulator (Manolis Savva* et al., 2019; Szot et al., 2021) enables continuous navigation on VLN (Krantz et al., 2020). AI2Thor is another virtual environment that enables object-interactive tasks. This is used in the instruction following task of ALFRED (Shridhar et al., 2020).

The final perspective is robotics. Among recent studies, SayCan (Ahn et al., 2022) uses large language models for ranking the possible action candidates during the episode, while Liang et al. (2022) uses large language models for decomposing instructions to perceptions and actions expressed in executable Python code format. Indeed, this perspective is still ongoing, and further elaborations are desired.

### 2.3 Interactive Robots (Yoshino)

When we focus on the interaction between robots and humans, from an engineering perspective, it is important to understand what robots can achieve in cooperation with humans. From a scientific perspective, it is also important to investigate the relationship between real-world nature, physicality, and linguistic expressions. For example, Visual Question Answering (VQA) (Antol et al., 2015) or Audio Visual Scene-aware Dialogue (AVSD) (D ' Haro et al., 2020; Alamri et al., 2019) is a typical case. Information exchange in a language tied (grounded) to the real world and interaction context is important for real-world language robotics. The use of multimodal data in the real world is important to solve this grounding challenge (Kottur et al., 2021). Discussions about the physicality of robots are also essential (Ahuja and Morency, 2019; Yazdian et al., 2022).

When we try to collaborate with a robot through actual interaction, the challenge is bridging the language interaction to real-world interaction, including actuation and grounding, using implicit knowledge or common sense about physical phenomena or social relationships (Xia et al., 2020). Conventionally such implicit knowledge is handcrafted as ontology; however, the building is costly because the robot requires prerequisite knowledge, common sense, and unspoken knowledge for each task and environment (Tanaka et al., 2023). Some recent works utilizing LLM indicate that LLMs can be used as such implicit world knowledge (Wu et al., 2023).

In addition to the above, there are still other research areas in robotics where language should play an important role, such as the robot's intentions, subjective experience (Yuguchi et al., 2022), desires and preferences, and memory mechanisms (Peller-Konrad et al., 2022). This tutorial will also discuss the future direction of language and robotics research.

## 3 Tutorial Format

Our tutorial consists of three lectures and one discussion. Each lecture has 40 mins talk with 10 mins short break from different viewpoints: language use in robotics, NLP in the real world, and interactive robots. After 30 mins coffee break, we will have a discussion about the future direction of the language and robotics research field.

During the lecture session, we open a question-answering form such as Dory, and participants put their questions and comments or vote for them. Based on the questions raised on the form, we have 40 mins open discussion with tutorial participants.

## 4 Reading List

This tutorial is introductory, and we do not assume special knowledge of participants if they have learned natural language processing. However, if you have never learned, reading papers about Transformer (Vaswani et al., 2017) and diffusion model (Ho et al., 2020) will emphasize your understanding. This tutorial will use the robot operating system 2 (ROS2). Online tutorial of ROS2[1] will emphasize your understanding.

## 5 Technical Requirements

We will use online communication systems such as Dory[2] to encourage discussion. It is expected to have devices that have internet access during the tutorial. We will open our slides and materials on our webpage[3] before the tutorial.

## 6 Instructors

We have three instructors from different research fields: robotics and control, vision and language, and human-robot interaction. The bibliography of each instructor follows.

### 6.1 Yutaka Nakamura

Yutaka Nakamura is a Team Leader at the Institute of Physical and Chemical Research (RIKEN) and an Affiliate Professor at Osaka University. He received his degree, Dr. Eng., from Nara Institute of Science and Technology (NAIST) in 2004. He worked at Osaka University as an assistant professor and an associate professor. Since 2020, he has

[1] `https://docs.ros.org/en/foxy/Tutorials.html`
[2] `https://dory.app`
[3] `https://github.com/riken-grp/langrobo-tutorial`

been working at Guardian Robot Project (GRP) of RIKEN as the team leader of Behavior Learning research team. He is working on areas of robotics, control, and human-robot interaction.

### 6.2 Shuhei Kurita

Shuhei Kurita is a Research Scientist at Center for Advanced Intelligence Project (AIP), RIKEN. He received his Ph.D. in informatics from Kyoto University in 2019. He is a visiting researcher in New York University for Assoc. Prof. Kyunghyun Cho from 2020. His paper "Neural Joint Model for Transition-based Chinese Syntactic Analysis"" was selected as the outstanding paper of ACL2017 (Kurita et al., 2017). He is working on natural language understanding in the real-world expressed in images, 3D scenes and photo-realistic simulator. He has actively published papers in natural language processing, learning representations and computer vision venues.

### 6.3 Koichiro Yoshino

Koichiro Yoshino is a Team Leader at the Institute of Physical and Chemical Research (RIKEN) and an Affiliate Professor at Nara Institute of Science and Technology (NAIST). He received his Ph.D. in informatics from Kyoto University in 2014. He worked at Kyoto University as a postdoc and at NAIST as an assistant professor. Since 2020, he has been working at Guardian Robot Project (GRP) of RIKEN as the team leader of Knowledge Acquisition and Dialogue research team. From 2019 to 2020, he was a visiting researcher at Heinrich-Heine-Universität Düsseldorf, Germany. He is working on spoken and natural language processing areas, especially robot dialogue systems. Dr. Koichiro Yoshino received several honors, including the best paper award of IWSDS2020 and the best paper award of the 1st NLP4ConvAI workshop. He is a member of IEEE Speech and Language Processing Technical Committee (SLTC), a member of Dialogue System Technology Challenge (DSTC) Steering Committee, an action editor of ACL Rolling Review (ARR), and a board member of SIGdial. He is a member of ACL, IEEE, SIGDIAL, IPSJ, JSAI, ANLP and RSJ.

## 7 Ethical Statement

Data used in Language and Robotics often contain personal identification codes such as facial images. The multimodal and interaction data used by the authors in this tutorial are discussed and reviewed by the ethics committee, if necessary, in accordance with the code of ethics of the organization to which they belong.

## References


Michael Ahn, Anthony Brohan, Noah Brown, Yevgen Chebotar, Omar Cortes, Byron David, Chelsea Finn, Chuyuan Fu, Keerthana Gopalakrishnan, Karol Hausman, Alex Herzog, Daniel Ho, Jasmine Hsu, Julian Ibarz, Brian Ichter, Alex Irpan, Eric Jang, Rosario Jauregui Ruano, Kyle Jeffrey, Sally Jesmonth, Nikhil Joshi, Ryan Julian, Dmitry Kalashnikov, Yuheng Kuang, Kuang-Huei Lee, Sergey Levine, Yao Lu, Linda Luu, Carolina Parada, Peter Pastor, Jornell Quiambao, Kanishka Rao, Jarek Rettinghouse, Diego Reyes, Pierre Sermanet, Nicolas Sievers, Clayton Tan, Alexander Toshev, Vincent Vanhoucke, Fei Xia, Ted Xiao, Peng Xu, Sichun Xu, Mengyuan Yan, and Andy Zeng. 2022. Do as i can and not as i say: Grounding language in robotic affordances. In *arXiv preprint arXiv:2204.01691*.

Chaitanya Ahuja and Louis-Philippe Morency. 2019. Language2pose: Natural language grounded pose forecasting. In *2019 International Conference on 3D Vision (3DV)*, pages 719–728. IEEE.

Huda Alamri, Vincent Cartillier, Abhishek Das, Jue Wang, Anoop Cherian, Irfan Essa, Dhruv Batra, Tim K Marks, Chiori Hori, Peter Anderson, et al. 2019. Audio visual scene-aware dialog. In *Proceedings of the IEEE/CVF Conference on Computer Vision and Pattern Recognition*, pages 7558–7567.

Peter Anderson, Qi Wu, Damien Teney, Jake Bruce, Mark Johnson, Niko Sünderhauf, Ian Reid, Stephen Gould, and Anton van den Hengel. 2018. Vision-and-Language Navigation: Interpreting visually-grounded navigation instructions in real environments. In *Proceedings of the IEEE Conference on Computer Vision and Pattern Recognition (CVPR)*.

Stanislaw Antol, Aishwarya Agrawal, Jiasen Lu, Margaret Mitchell, Dhruv Batra, C Lawrence Zitnick, and Devi Parikh. 2015. Vqa: Visual question answering. In *Proceedings of the IEEE international conference on computer vision*, pages 2425–2433.

Daichi Azuma, Taiki Miyanishi, Shuhei Kurita, and Motoki Kawanabe. 2022. Scanqa: 3d question answering for spatial scene understanding. In *Proceedings of the IEEE/CVF Conference on Computer Vision and Pattern Recognition (CVPR)*.

Raffaella Bernardi, Ruket Cakici, Desmond Elliott, Aykut Erdem, Erkut Erdem, Nazli Ikizler-Cinbis, Frank Keller, Adrian Muscat, and Barbara Plank. 2016. Automatic description generation from images: A survey of models, datasets, and evaluation measures. 55(1):409–442.

Anthony Brohan, Noah Brown, Justice Carbajal, Yevgen Chebotar, Joseph Dabis, Chelsea Finn, Keerthana Gopalakrishnan, Karol Hausman, Alex Herzog, Jasmine Hsu, et al. 2022. Rt-1: Robotics transformer for real-world control at scale. *arXiv preprint arXiv:2212.06817*.

Anthony Brohan, Yevgen Chebotar, Chelsea Finn, Karol Hausman, Alexander Herzog, Daniel Ho, Julian Ibarz, Alex Irpan, Eric Jang, Ryan Julian, et al. 2023. Do as i can, not as i say: Grounding language in robotic affordances. In *Conference on Robot Learning*, pages 287–318. PMLR.

Angel Chang, Angela Dai, Thomas Funkhouser, Maciej Halber, Matthias Niessner, Manolis Savva, Shuran Song, Andy Zeng, and Yinda Zhang. 2017. Matterport3D: Learning from RGB-D data in indoor environments. *International Conference on 3D Vision (3DV)*.

Dave Zhenyu Chen, Angel X Chang, and Matthias Nießner. 2020. Scanrefer: 3d object localization in rgb-d scans using natural language. *16th European Conference on Computer Vision (ECCV)*.

Angela Dai, Angel X. Chang, Manolis Savva, Maciej Halber, Thomas Funkhouser, and Matthias Nießner. 2017. Scannet: Richly-annotated 3d reconstructions of indoor scenes. In *Proc. Computer Vision and Pattern Recognition (CVPR), IEEE*.

Luis Fernando D'Haro, Koichiro Yoshino, Chiori Hori, Tim K Marks, Lazaros Polymenakos, Jonathan K Kummerfeld, Michel Galley, and Xiang Gao. 2020. Overview of the seventh dialog system technology challenge: Dstc7. *Computer Speech & Language*, 62:101068.

Richard E Fikes and Nils J Nilsson. 1971. Strips: A new approach to the application of theorem proving to problem solving. *Artificial intelligence*, 2(3-4):189–208.

Maria Fox and Derek Long. 2003. Pddl2. 1: An extension to pddl for expressing temporal planning domains. *Journal of artificial intelligence research*, 20:61–124.

Daniel Fried, Ronghang Hu, Volkan Cirik, Anna Rohrbach, Jacob Andreas, Louis-Philippe Morency, Taylor Berg-Kirkpatrick, Kate Saenko, Dan Klein, and Trevor Darrell. 2018. Speaker-follower models for vision-and-language navigation. In S. Bengio, H. Wallach, H. Larochelle, K. Grauman, N. Cesa-Bianchi, and R. Garnett, editors, *Advances in Neural Information Processing Systems 31*, pages 3314–3325. Curran Associates, Inc.

Kristen Grauman, Andrew Westbury, Eugene Byrne, Zachary Chavis, Antonino Furnari, Rohit Girdhar, Jackson Hamburger, Hao Jiang, Miao Liu, Xingyu Liu, Miguel Martin, Tushar Nagarajan, Ilija Radosavovic, Santhosh Kumar Ramakrishnan, Fiona Ryan, Jayant Sharma, Michael Wray, Mengmeng Xu, Eric Zhongcong Xu, Chen Zhao, Siddhant Bansal, Dhruv Batra, Vincent Cartillier, Sean Crane, Tien Do, Morrie Doulaty, Akshay Erapalli, Christoph Feichtenhofer, Adriano Fragomeni, Qichen Fu, Christian Fuegen, Abrham Gebreselasie, Cristina Gonzalez, James Hillis, Xuhua Huang, Yifei Huang, Wenqi Jia, Weslie Khoo, Jachym Kolar, Satwik Kottur, Anurag Kumar, Federico Landini, Chao Li, Yanghao Li, Zhenqiang Li, Karttikeya Mangalam, Raghava Modhugu, Jonathan Munro, Tullie Murrell, Takumi Nishiyasu, Will Price, Paola Ruiz Puentes, Merey Ramazanova, Leda Sari, Kiran Somasundaram, Audrey Southerland, Yusuke Sugano, Ruijie Tao, Minh Vo, Yuchen Wang, Xindi Wu, Takuma Yagi, Yunyi Zhu, Pablo Arbelaez, David Crandall, Dima Damen, Giovanni Maria Farinella, Bernard Ghanem, Vamsi Krishna Ithapu, C. V. Jawahar, Hanbyul Joo, Kris Kitani, Haizhou Li, Richard Newcombe, Aude Oliva, Hyun Soo Park, James M. Rehg, Yoichi Sato, Jianbo Shi, Mike Zheng Shou, Antonio Torralba, Lorenzo Torresani, Mingfei Yan, and Jitendra Malik. 2022. Ego4d: Around the World in 3,000 Hours of Egocentric Video. In *Proceedings of the IEEE/CVF Computer Vision and Pattern Recognition (CVPR)*.

Weituo Hao, Chunyuan Li, Xiujun Li, Lawrence Carin, and Jianfeng Gao. 2020. Towards learning a generic agent for vision-and-language navigation via pre-training. *Conference on Computer Vision and Pattern Recognition (CVPR)*.

Jun Hatori, Yuta Kikuchi, Sosuke Kobayashi, Kuniyuki Takahashi, Yuta Tsuboi, Yuya Unno, Wilson Ko, and Jethro Tan. 2018. Interactively picking real-world objects with unconstrained spoken language instructions. In *2018 IEEE International Conference on Robotics and Automation (ICRA)*, pages 3774–3781. IEEE.

Jonathan Ho, Ajay Jain, and Pieter Abbeel. 2020. Denoising diffusion probabilistic models. *Advances in Neural Information Processing Systems*, 33:6840–6851.

Sahar Kazemzadeh, Vicente Ordonez, Mark Matten, and Tamara Berg. 2014. ReferItGame: Referring to objects in photographs of natural scenes. In *Proceedings of the Conference on Empirical Methods in Natural Language Processing (EMNLP)*.

Satwik Kottur, Seungwhan Moon, Alborz Geramifard, and Babak Damavandi. 2021. Simmc 2.0: A task-oriented dialog dataset for immersive multimodal conversations. In *Proceedings of the 2021 Conference on Empirical Methods in Natural Language Processing*, pages 4903–4912.

Jacob Krantz, Erik Wijmans, Arjun Majundar, Dhruv Batra, and Stefan Lee. 2020. Beyond the nav-graph: Vision and language navigation in continuous environments. In *European Conference on Computer Vision (ECCV)*.

Shuhei Kurita and Kyunghyun Cho. 2021. Generative language-grounded policy in vision-and-language navigation with bayes' rule. In *International Conference on Learning Representations (ICLR)*.

Shuhei Kurita, Daisuke Kawahara, and Sadao Kurohashi. 2017. Neural joint model for transition-based Chinese syntactic analysis. In *Proceedings of the 55th Annual Meeting of the Association for Computational Linguistics (Volume 1: Long Papers)*, pages 1204–1214, Vancouver, Canada. Association for Computational Linguistics.

Jacky Liang, Wenlong Huang, Fei Xia, Peng Xu, Karol Hausman, Brian Ichter, Pete Florence, and Andy Zeng. 2022. Code as policies: Language model programs for embodied control. In *arXiv preprint arXiv:2209.07753*.

Manolis Savva*, Abhishek Kadian*, Oleksandr Maksymets*, Yili Zhao, Erik Wijmans, Bhavana Jain, Julian Straub, Jia Liu, Vladlen Koltun, Jitendra Malik, Devi Parikh, and Dhruv Batra. 2019. Habitat: A Platform for Embodied AI Research. In *Proceedings of the IEEE/CVF International Conference on Computer Vision (ICCV)*.

Junhua Mao, Jonathan Huang, Alexander Toshev, Oana Camburu, Alan Yuille, and Kevin Murphy. 2016. Generation and Comprehension of Unambiguous Object Descriptions. In *Proceedings of the IEEE Conference on Computer Vision and Pattern Recognition (CVPR)*.

Fabian Peller-Konrad, Christian RG Dreher, Andre Meixner, Fabian Reister, Markus Grotz, Tamim Asfour, et al. 2022. Conceptual design of the memory system of the robot cognitive architecture armarx. *arXiv preprint arXiv:2206.02241*.

Bryan A. Plummer, Liwei Wang, Chris M. Cervantes, Juan C. Caicedo, Julia Hockenmaier, and Svetlana Lazebnik. 2015. Flickr30k Entities: Collecting Region-to-Phrase Correspondences for Richer Image-to-Sentence Models. In *Proceedings of the IEEE International Conference on Computer Vision (ICCV)*.

Scott Reed, Konrad Zolna, Emilio Parisotto, Sergio Gómez Colmenarejo, Alexander Novikov, Gabriel Barth-maron, Mai Giménez, Yury Sulsky, Jackie Kay, Jost Tobias Springenberg, et al. A generalist agent. *Transactions on Machine Learning Research*.

Mohit Shridhar, Jesse Thomason, Daniel Gordon, Yonatan Bisk, Winson Han, Roozbeh Mottaghi, Luke Zettlemoyer, and Dieter Fox. 2020. ALFRED: A Benchmark for Interpreting Grounded Instructions for Everyday Tasks. In *The IEEE Conference on Computer Vision and Pattern Recognition (CVPR)*.

Andrew Szot, Alex Clegg, Eric Undersander, Erik Wijmans, Yili Zhao, John Turner, Noah Maestre, Mustafa Mukadam, Devendra Chaplot, Oleksandr Maksymets, Aaron Gokaslan, Vladimir Vondrus, Sameer Dharur, Franziska Meier, Wojciech Galuba, Angel Chang, Zsolt Kira, Vladlen Koltun, Jitendra Malik, Manolis Savva, and Dhruv Batra. 2021. Habitat 2.0: Training home assistants to rearrange their habitat. In *Advances in Neural Information Processing Systems (NeurIPS)*.

Hao Tan, Licheng Yu, and Mohit Bansal. 2019. Learning to navigate unseen environments: Back translation with environmental dropout. In *Proceedings of the 2019 Conference of the North American Chapter of the Association for Computational Linguistics: Human Language Technologies, Volume 1 (Long and Short Papers)*, pages 2610–2621, Minneapolis, Minnesota. Association for Computational Linguistics.

Shohei Tanaka, Koichiro Yoshino, Katsuhito Sudoh, and Satoshi Nakamura. 2023. Reflective action selection based on positive-unlabeled learning and causality detection model. *Computer Speech & Language*, 78:101463.

Guy Tevet, Sigal Raab, Brian Gordon, Yonatan Shafir, Daniel Cohen-Or, and Amit H Bermano. 2022. Human motion diffusion model. *arXiv preprint arXiv:2209.14916*.

Ashish Vaswani, Noam Shazeer, Niki Parmar, Jakob Uszkoreit, Llion Jones, Aidan N Gomez, Łukasz Kaiser, and Illia Polosukhin. 2017. Attention is all you need. *Advances in neural information processing systems*, 30.

Jimmy Wu, Rika Antonova, Adam Kan, Marion Lepert, Andy Zeng, Shuran Song, Jeannette Bohg, Szymon Rusinkiewicz, and Thomas Funkhouser. 2023. Tidybot: Personalized robot assistance with large language models. *arXiv preprint arXiv:2305.05658*.

Fei Xia, William B Shen, Chengshu Li, Priya Kasimbeg, Micael Edmond Tchapmi, Alexander Toshev, Roberto Martín-Martín, and Silvio Savarese. 2020. Interactive gibson benchmark: A benchmark for interactive navigation in cluttered environments. *IEEE Robotics and Automation Letters*, 5(2):713–720.

Payam Jome Yazdian, Mo Chen, and Angelica Lim. 2022. Gesture2vec: Clustering gestures using representation learning methods for co-speech gesture generation. In *2022 IEEE/RSJ International Conference on Intelligent Robots and Systems (IROS)*, pages 3100–3107. IEEE.

Licheng Yu, Patrick Poirson, Shan Yang, Alexander C. Berg, and Tamara L. Berg. 2016. Modeling Context in Referring Expressions. In *Proceedings of the European Conference on Computer Vision (ECCV)*.

Akishige Yuguchi, Seiya Kawano, Koichiro Yoshino, Carlos Toshinori Ishi, Yasutomo Kawanishi, Yutaka Nakamura, Takashi Minato, Yasuki Saito, and

Michihiko Minoh. 2022. Butsukusa: A conversational mobile robot describing its own observations and internal states. In *2022 17th ACM/IEEE International Conference on Human-Robot Interaction (HRI)*, pages 1114–1118. IEEE.

# Current Status of NLP in South East Asia with Insights from Multilingualism and Language Diversity

**Alham Fikri Aji**[*α], **Jessica Zosa Forde**[*β], **Alyssa Marie Loo**[*β], **Lintang Sutawika**[*γ], **Skyler Wang**[*δ,ϵ], **Genta Indra Winata**[*η], **Zheng-Xin Yong**[*β], **Ruochen Zhang**[*β], **A. Seza Doğruöz**[*κ], **Yin Lin Tan**[*λ,π], **Jan Christian Blaise Cruz**[*ϕ]

[α]MBZUAI [β]Brown University [γ]EleutherAI [δ]UC Berkeley
[ϵ] Meta AI [η]Bloomberg [κ]Ghent University [λ]Stanford University
[π]National University of Singapore [ϕ]Samsung R&D Institute Philippines

## 1 Motivation & Objectives

South East Asia (SEA) is a region with immense cultural and linguistic diversity—a melting pot of cultures, religions, and languages and it has a linguistic diversity hosting over 1000 languages (Table 1). In addition, multilingualism (i.e., speaking more than one language or dialect) is widely practiced on a daily basis. Despite the variety of languages, there is relatively less research on natural language processing (NLP) of the languages and their users in the area compared to languages in other regions. Many low-resource languages in the region will face potential endangerment in the long run.[1]

| Country | Population | # Languages |
|---|---|---|
| Brunei | 0.5M | 16 |
| Cambodia | 17M | 28 |
| Indonesia | 267M | 711 |
| Laos | 7M | 87 |
| Malaysia | 32M | 131 |
| Myanmar | 54M | 121 |
| Philippines | 109M | 184 |
| Singapore | 6M | 24 |
| Thailand | 70M | 73 |
| Timor-Leste | 1M | 22 |
| Vietnam | 96M | 110 |

Table 1: Language and population statistics of SEA countries, according to Ethnologue (Eberhard et al., 2021).

A significant challenge facing SEA NLP is the scarcity of available datasets and benchmarks for the region's languages, many of which are low-resource, resulting in sub-optimal performance of models. Similar to the situation in India, Europe, and Africa, most language users in SEA are multilingual; code-switching is common (Doğruöz et al., 2021; Winata et al., 2022b; Yong et al., 2023b) and it should not be seen as a challenge but as the natural way of communication in these settings. Language technology may also not be accessible to certain groups of SEA researchers due to the constraints on computing resources, hardware, training, and funding.

This tutorial will present an overview of language issues in the SEA region, link multilingualism and computational sociolinguistics with historical and societal perspectives, and provide a summary of the existing datasets for computational linguistics research, NLP systems, and evaluation benchmarks. Our goal is to inform the AACL'23 audience about challenges and opportunities for NLP research in SEA, taking the linguistic diversity in the region and multilingualism among the users and communities into account, while providing an overview of current NLP research on the languages spoken in the area. By providing an overview, we will highlight the research gaps to be tackled in the future.

## 2 Type of Tutorial

This is a three-hour long **introductory** tutorial. The number of NLP publications focusing on SEA languages have been steadily increasing in recent years, but there is no tutorial at international venues (e.g., ACL/EMNLP/NAACL/EACL/COLING) that has systematically reviewed this research.

## 3 Target Audience and Prerequisites

This tutorial targets both junior and senior researchers (including NLP practitioners and lin-

*Equal contribution.

[1] https://www.ethnologue.com/region/SEA



*Proceedings of the 13th International Joint Conference on Natural Language Processing and the 3rd Conference of the Asia-Pacific Chapter of the Association for Computational Linguistics (Tutorial Abstracts)*, pages 8–13
November 1–4, 2023. ©2023 Association for Computational Linguistics

guists) who are broadly interested in multilingual NLP and want to gain a deeper understanding of multilingualism work in the area as well as NLP research for SEA languages. Since this AACL 2023 tutorial takes place in Bali, Indonesia, where the location matches our tutorial topic, we foresee a substantial number of researchers from the SEA region attending the tutorial. We assume the audience has no previous knowledge about linguistics, multilingualism, and/or NLP in SEA. We expect that most participants will be familiar with basic issues in modeling language and in standard methods for learning from data, but no specific knowledge will be assumed.

## 4 Outline of Tutorial Content

The tutorial will cover four parts over the course of three hours:

1. Introduction to SEA (15 minutes)
2. Linguistic Landscape and Multilingualism in the SEA region (75 minutes)
3. Resource Availability and Collection (60 minutes)
4. (Panel Discussion) Research Ecosystem (30 minutes)

### 4.1 Introduction to SEA

We will start our tutorial by introducing SEA through discussing its geography, history, and culture. The topics here will be set the groundwork for what multilingualism means for SEA region, including its linguistic diversity and available resources.

### 4.2 Linguistic Landscape and Multilingualism in the SEA region

We will provide an overview of the language situation in SEA. We will begin by exploring the diversity of languages and language families in the region. The perspective of sociolinguistics, historical, and societal will be presented (Doğruöz and Sitaram, 2022). The multilingual nature of SEA will be highlighted through a discussion of language variation both between-country. Lastly, we will also briefly touch on language policies that have shaped the linguistic landscape of the SEA countries.

### 4.3 Resource Availability and Collection

We will discuss the availability of datasets, including unlabeled raw text corpora and labeled task-specific datasets, as well as the challenges of collecting, maintaining, and annotating these datasets. Additionally, we will explore where these datasets can be accessed, how various SEA countries organize their NLP resources, and to what extent they accurately represent common linguistic phenomena in SEA countries, such as code-switching and multilingualism.

Moreover, we will provide an overview of pretrained language models for SEA languages. We will delve into how these models are linguistically motivated by the multilingual society and how the'y are designed to address different linguistic challenges in various SEA countries.

Lastly, we will introduce existing benchmark tasks for evaluating the pretrained models and touch upon the current shortcomings of the available NLP resources.

### 4.4 Research Ecosystem

Finally, through a panel discussion, we will discuss the meta-environment situating NLP research in SEA, including potential research collaborations and opportunities across SEA regions (Rungta et al., 2022) and the uneven distribution of research resources. We will highlight some community-based initiatives working on SEA languages. We will also involve the audience when sharing our research experience, highlighting the challenges as well as the opportunities for developing NLP technologies for SEA languages.

## 5 Breadth of the Tutorial

The tutorial covers a diverse set of topics related to NLP for SEA languages including their linguistics, data, models, evaluation, open research questions, etc. The tutorial also discusses the state of NLP research in different SEA regions.

## 6 Diversity Considerations

**Instructors** Our team spans across various (i) backgrounds and connections to SEA (ii) types of institutions, including academia, start-ups, and established tech companies, (iii) geographic locations, and (iv) seniority levels, gender and sexual identities.

**Scope** We introduce datasets, tasks, and NLP models that cover many SEA languages (including their dialects) from different language families.

**Audience** We target audiences interested in SEA languages from both academia and industry. We also welcome researchers who have worked with various SEA languages to share their challenges and experience during the panel discussion to foster an inclusive environment.

## 7 Reading List

The recommended reading list is as follows.

### 7.1 General Background

The following papers give a high-level overview of available resources, linguistic characteristics, and language technologies related to our tutorial.

1. One Country, 700+ Languages: NLP Challenges for Underrepresented Languages and Dialects in Indonesia. (Aji et al., 2022)

2. A Survey of Code-switching: Linguistic and Social Perspectives for Language Technologies (Doğruöz et al., 2021)

3. Language Technologies for Low Resource Languages: Sociolinguistic and Multilingual Insights. (Doğruöz and Sitaram, 2022)

4. Survey on Thai NLP Language Resources and Tools. (Arreerard et al., 2022)

5. Areal Linguistics and Mainland SEA (Enfield, 2005)

6. No Language Left Behind: Scaling Human-Centered Machine Translation (NLLB Team et al., 2022)

### 7.2 Resource Collection and Availability

The following papers characterize efforts in curating labeled datasets and organizing benchmark evaluation for SEA languages as well as training language models.

#### 7.2.1 Datasets and Evaluation

1. Crowdsourcing-based Annotation of Emotions in Filipino and English Tweets. (Lapitan et al., 2016)

2. SEAME: a Mandarin-English Code-switching Speech Corpus in SEA (Lyu et al., 2010)

3. NusaX: Multilingual Parallel Sentiment Dataset for 10 Indonesian Local Languages. (Winata et al., 2023)

4. Cross-lingual Few-Shot Learning on Unseen Languages. (Winata et al., 2022a)

5. NusaCrowd: Open Source Initiative for Indonesian NLP Resources (Cahyawijaya et al., 2023)

6. BRCC and SentiBahasaRojak: The First Bahasa Rojak Corpus for Pretraining and Sentiment Analysis Dataset (Romadhona et al., 2022)

#### 7.2.2 Pretrained Language Models

1. IndoLEM and IndoBERT: A Benchmark Dataset and Pre-trained Language Model for Indonesian NLP. (Koto et al., 2020)

2. PhoBERT: Pre-trained language models for Vietnamese. (Nguyen and Tuan Nguyen, 2020)

3. WangchanBERTa: Pretraining transformer-based Thai Language Models (Lowphansirikul et al., 2021)

4. Encoder-Decoder Language Model for Khmer Handwritten Text Recognition in Historical Documents (Born et al., 2022)

5. LaoPLM: Pre-trained Language Models for Lao. (Lin et al., 2022)

6. Tagalog RoBERTa: Improving Large Scale Language Models and Resources for Filipino. (Cruz and Cheng, 2022)

## 8 Sharing of Tutorial Materials

All of our tutorial materials will be publicly available at `https://aacl2023-sea-nlp.github.io`.

## 9 Ethics Statement

Preserving multilingualism and directing attention to low-resource languages is a pertinent collective mission in NLP research today. As prominent projects like "No Language Left Behind" (NLLB Team et al., 2022) argue, prioritizing high-resource languages comes with the cost of under-privileging research on low-resource languages. As a result of linguistic inequality, large language models contain cross-lingual vulnerability (Yong et al., 2023a), and low-resource languages could face endangerment, where useful resources that could be developed for these language speakers may never materialize. Furthermore, as many SEA NLP researchers speak high-resource languages, existing academic practices and cultures may compel them to focus on these languages rather than their low-resource counterparts. The uneven distribution of research resources, such as hardware, training, and funding, may also present hurdles for interested researchers to develop NLP systems for SEA languages. Ultimately, we recognize that many low-resource SEA languages remain understudied due to a confluence of reasons, and it is our hope that this tutorial could spark productive conversations around how we can bring sustained attention to this area of research.

## 10 Presenter Information

**Alham Fikri Aji** is an assistant professor in MBZUAI. His research focuses on multi-lingual and cross-lingual NLP, especially for under-resourced languages and communities. His work area also includes data construction as well as data-efficient systems, and compute-efficient models for better accessibility. His email is alham.fikri@mbzuai.ac.ae.

**Jessica Zosa Forde** is a PhD Candidate at Brown University. Jessica's research focuses on the evaluation of deep learning models, to improve their reliability in high stakes domains. Jessica presented a tutorial on reproduciblity in NLP at ACL in 2022. Her email is jessica_forde@brown.edu.

**Alyssa Marie Loo** is an undergraduate in Linguistics and Computer Science at Brown University. Her research focuses on interpretability of large language models and their alignment with human linguistic behavior. Her email is alyssa_loo@brown.edu.

**Lintang Sutawika** is Researcher at EleutherAI. He is a proponent of open source software and machine learning artifacts. His work has comprised of extending language models to more languages, interpreting language models and maintaining software for language model evaluation. His email is lintang@eleuther.ai

**Samson Tan** is an Applied Scientist at AWS AI Research & Education. His research focuses on linguistic variation and their effect on the robustness and evaluation of NLP models. His email is samson@amazon.com.

**Skyler Wang** is a PhD Candidate at UC Berkeley and a Visiting Sociologist at Meta AI. Broadly, Skyler's research focuses on creating socially and ethically-grounded machine translation technologies for low-resource language communities. He is a Sociologist on Meta AI's "No Language Left Behind" team. His email is skyler.wang@berkeley.edu.

**Genta Indra Winata** is a Senior Research Scientist at Bloomberg. His research focuses on multilingual, cross-lingual, language models, dialogue system, and low-resource NLP. His work area includes few-shot learning and evaluation of large language models. His email is gwinata@bloomberg.net.

**Zheng-Xin Yong** is a PhD Candidate at Brown University. His research focuses on cross-lingual NLP, large language models, and AI safety. His email is contact.yong@brown.edu

**Ruochen Zhang** is a PhD Candidate at Brown University. Her research interests lie in multi-/cross-lingual learning, evaluation and application of large language models. Her email is ruochen_zhang@brown.edu.

**A. Seza Doğruöz** is a tenured Associate Professor at Ghent University. She conducts interdisciplinary research on multilingualism, sociolinguistics and computational linguistics. Her email is as.dogruoz@ugent.be.

**Yin Lin Tan** is a PhD student at Stanford University. Her research focuses on sociolinguistic variation, phonetics, and multilingualism. Her email is yltan@stanford.edu.

**Jan Christian Blaise Cruz** is an AI Research Engineer at Samsung R&D Institute Philippines. His research revolves around low-resource techniques for translation and language generation. His email is jcb.cruz@samsung.com.

## References


Alham Fikri Aji, Genta Indra Winata, Fajri Koto, Samuel Cahyawijaya, Ade Romadhony, Rahmad Mahendra, Kemal Kurniawan, David Moeljadi, Radityo Eko Prasojo, Timothy Baldwin, Jey Han Lau, and Sebastian Ruder. 2022. One country, 700+ languages: NLP challenges for underrepresented languages and dialects in Indonesia. In *Proceedings of the 60th Annual Meeting of the Association for Computational Linguistics (Volume 1: Long Papers)*, pages 7226–7249, Dublin, Ireland. Association for Computational Linguistics.

Ratchakrit Arreerard, Stephen Mander, and Scott Piao. 2022. Survey on Thai NLP language resources and tools. In *Proceedings of the Thirteenth Language Resources and Evaluation Conference*, pages 6495–6505, Marseille, France. European Language Resources Association.

Seanghort Born, Dona Valy, and Phutphalla Kong. 2022. Encoder-decoder language model for khmer handwritten text recognition in historical documents. In *2022 14th International Conference on Software, Knowledge, Information Management and Applications (SKIMA)*, pages 234–238.

Samuel Cahyawijaya, Holy Lovenia, Alham Fikri Aji, Genta Winata, Bryan Wilie, Fajri Koto, Rahmad Mahendra, Christian Wibisono, Ade Romadhony, Karissa Vincentio, Jennifer Santoso, David Moeljadi, Cahya Wirawan, Frederikus Hudi, Muhammad Satrio Wicaksono, Ivan Parmonangan, Ika Alfina, Ilham Firdausi Putra, Samsul Rahmadani, Yulianti Oenang, Ali Septiandri, James Jaya, Kaustubh Dhole, Arie Suryani, Rifki Afina Putri, Dan Su, Keith Stevens, Made Nindyatama Nityasya, Muhammad Adilazuarda, Ryan Hadiwijaya, Ryandito Diandaru, Tiezheng Yu, Vito Ghifari, Wenliang Dai, Yan Xu, Dyah Damapuspita, Haryo Wibowo, Cuk Tho, Ichwanul Karo Karo, Tirana Fatyanosa, Ziwei Ji, Graham Neubig, Timothy Baldwin, Sebastian Ruder, Pascale Fung, Herry Sujaini, Sakriani Sakti, and Ayu Purwarianti. 2023. NusaCrowd: Open source initiative for Indonesian NLP resources. In *Findings of the Association for Computational Linguistics: ACL 2023*, pages 13745–13818, Toronto, Canada. Association for Computational Linguistics.

Jan Christian Blaise Cruz and Charibeth Cheng. 2022. Improving large-scale language models and resources for Filipino. In *Proceedings of the Thirteenth Language Resources and Evaluation Conference*, pages 6548–6555, Marseille, France. European Language Resources Association.

A. Seza Doğruöz and Sunayana Sitaram. 2022. Language technologies for low resource languages: Sociolinguistic and multilingual insights. In *Proceedings of the 1st Annual Meeting of the ELRA/ISCA Special Interest Group on Under-Resourced Languages*, pages 92–97, Marseille, France. European Language Resources Association.

A. Seza Doğruöz, Sunayana Sitaram, Barbara E. Bullock, and Almeida Jacqueline Toribio. 2021. A survey of code-switching: Linguistic and social perspectives for language technologies. In *Proceedings of the 59th Annual Meeting of the Association for Computational Linguistics and the 11th International Joint Conference on Natural Language Processing (Volume 1: Long Papers)*, pages 1654–1666, Online. Association for Computational Linguistics.

David M. Eberhard, Gary F. Simons, and Charles D. Fennig. 2021. *Ethnologue: Languages of the World. Twenty-fourth edition.* Dallas, Texas: SIL International.

Nick J Enfield. 2005. Areal linguistics and mainland southeast asia. *Annual review of anthropology*, 34:181–206.

Fajri Koto, Afshin Rahimi, Jey Han Lau, and Timothy Baldwin. 2020. IndoLEM and IndoBERT: A benchmark dataset and pre-trained language model for Indonesian NLP. In *Proceedings of the 28th International Conference on Computational Linguistics*, pages 757–770, Barcelona, Spain (Online). International Committee on Computational Linguistics.

Fermin Roberto Lapitan, Riza Theresa Batista-Navarro, and Eliezer Albacea. 2016. Crowdsourcing-based annotation of emotions in Filipino and English tweets. In *Proceedings of the 6th Workshop on South and Southeast Asian Natural Language Processing (WSSANLP2016)*, pages 74–82, Osaka, Japan. The COLING 2016 Organizing Committee.

Nankai Lin, Yingwen Fu, Chuwei Chen, Ziyu Yang, and Shengyi Jiang. 2022. LaoPLM: Pre-trained language models for Lao. In *Proceedings of the Thirteenth Language Resources and Evaluation Conference*, pages 6506–6512, Marseille, France. European Language Resources Association.

Lalita Lowphansirikul, Charin Polpanumas, Nawat Jantrakulchai, and Sarana Nutanong. 2021. Wangchanberta: Pretraining transformer-based thai language models. *arXiv preprint arXiv:2101.09635*.

Dau-Cheng Lyu, Tien-Ping Tan, Eng Siong Chng, and Haizhou Li. 2010. Seame: a mandarin-english code-switching speech corpus in south-east asia. In *Eleventh Annual Conference of the International Speech Communication Association*.

Dat Quoc Nguyen and Anh Tuan Nguyen. 2020. PhoBERT: Pre-trained language models for Vietnamese. In *Findings of the Association for Computational Linguistics: EMNLP 2020*, pages 1037–1042, Online. Association for Computational Linguistics.

NLLB Team, Marta R. Costa-jussà, James Cross, Onur Çelebi, Maha Elbayad, Kenneth Heafield, Kevin Heffernan, Elahe Kalbassi, Janice Lam, Daniel Licht, Jean Maillard, Anna Sun, Skyler Wang, Guillaume Wenzek, Al Youngblood, Bapi Akula, Loic Barrault, Gabriel Mejia Gonzalez, Prangthip Hansanti,

John Hoffman, Semarley Jarrett, Kaushik Ram Sadagopan, Dirk Rowe, Shannon Spruit, Chau Tran, Pierre Andrews, Necip Fazil Ayan, Shruti Bhosale, Sergey Edunov, Angela Fan, Cynthia Gao, Vedanuj Goswami, Francisco Guzmán, Philipp Koehn, Alexandre Mourachko, Christophe Ropers, Safiyyah Saleem, Holger Schwenk, and Jeff Wang. 2022. No language left behind: Scaling human-centered machine translation. *arxiv preprint arxiv:2207.04672*.

Nanda Putri Romadhona, Sin-En Lu, Bo-Han Lu, and Richard Tzong-Han Tsai. 2022. BRCC and SentiBahasaRojak: The first Bahasa rojak corpus for pretraining and sentiment analysis dataset. In *Proceedings of the 29th International Conference on Computational Linguistics*, pages 4418–4428, Gyeongju, Republic of Korea. International Committee on Computational Linguistics.

Mukund Rungta, Janvijay Singh, Saif M Mohammad, and Diyi Yang. 2022. Geographic citation gaps in nlp research. *arXiv preprint arXiv:2210.14424*.

Genta Winata, Shijie Wu, Mayank Kulkarni, Thamar Solorio, and Daniel Preoţiuc-Pietro. 2022a. Cross-lingual few-shot learning on unseen languages. In *Proceedings of the 2nd Conference of the Asia-Pacific Chapter of the Association for Computational Linguistics and the 12th International Joint Conference on Natural Language Processing*, pages 777–791.

Genta Indra Winata, Alham Fikri Aji, Samuel Cahyawijaya, Rahmad Mahendra, Fajri Koto, Ade Romadhony, Kemal Kurniawan, David Moeljadi, Radityo Eko Prasojo, Pascale Fung, Timothy Baldwin, Jey Han Lau, Rico Sennrich, and Sebastian Ruder. 2023. NusaX: Multilingual parallel sentiment dataset for 10 Indonesian local languages. In *Proceedings of the 17th Conference of the European Chapter of the Association for Computational Linguistics*, pages 815–834, Dubrovnik, Croatia. Association for Computational Linguistics.

Genta Indra Winata, Alham Fikri Aji, Zheng-Xin Yong, and Thamar Solorio. 2022b. The decades progress on code-switching research in nlp: A systematic survey on trends and challenges. *arXiv preprint arXiv:2212.09660*.

Zheng-Xin Yong, Cristina Menghini, and Stephen H. Bach. 2023a. Low-resource languages jailbreak gpt-4. *arXiv preprint arXiv:2310.02446*.

Zheng-Xin Yong, Ruochen Zhang, Jessica Zosa Forde, Skyler Wang, Samuel Cahyawijaya, Holy Lovenia, Genta Indra Winata, Lintang Sutawika, Jan Christian Blaise Cruz, Long Phan, Yin Lin Tan, and Alham Fikri Aji. 2023b. Prompting multilingual large language models to generate code-mixed texts: The case of south east asian languages.

# Practical Tools from Domain Adaptation for Designing Inclusive, Equitable, and Robust Generative AI


**Anthony Sicilia**
Khoury College of Computer Sciences
Northeastern University
sicilia.a@northeastern.edu

**Malihe Alikhani**
Khoury College of Computer Sciences
Northeastern University
m.alikhani@northeastern.edu



## Abstract

Generative language technologies have become integral to everyday communication, shaping social interactions and informing critical decision-making processes in areas such as recruitment, healthcare, and education. However, they often struggle to grasp the "long tail" of data distributions — concepts less frequently observed during training — which could have significant repercussions. These models may marginalize underrepresented groups by failing to comprehend preferred communication styles, such as code-switching, or perpetuating societal biases like gender bias. Sectors like healthcare, education, and law, requiring personalization and exhibiting nuanced linguistic features, are also particularly affected when pre-trained models misconstrue or overlook "long tail" data concepts. While methods like distillation of smaller language models, active learning, and other bias mitigation strategies can augment traditional training techniques, a careful statistical analysis is essential for their effective application. This tutorial offers a comprehensive examination of how to develop equitable, robust, and inclusive language technologies using statistical tools from Domain Adaptation (DA) that catalyze positive social change. We will delve into strategies for bias mitigation, explore how to measure bias, and examine open problems in creating culturally-grounded and inclusive language technologies. Accompanying code notebooks and packages will be provided.[1]


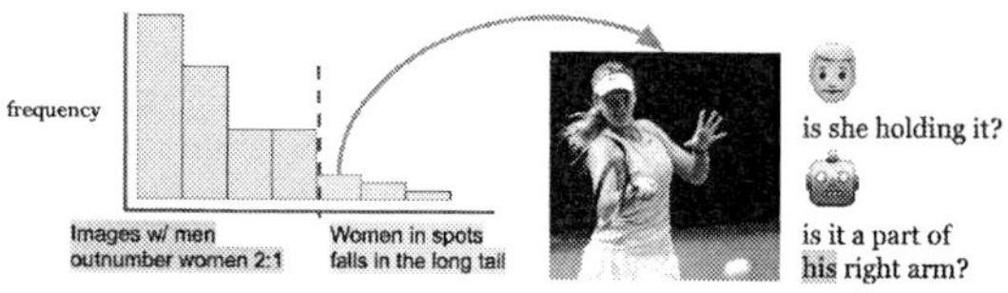


Figure 1: DA theory quantifies key properties of text data to inform us about model generalization; e.g., it can identify the long tail to promote equitable text generation for underrepresented groups.

## 1 Introduction

Large language models are increasingly deployed in critical areas of our daily life. Applications can improve health literacy (Ufuk, 2023), offer new avenues for improved education (Kasneci et al., 2023), and yield new legal technologies (Chalkidis et al., 2020). Meanwhile, as the complexity of these models increases, robust decision making, algorithm design, and evaluation become more and more important. It is vital that under-served demographics are not left behind in the wake of this technological wave – e.g., by supporting user-specific behaviors like code-switching (Harrington and Egede, 2023), low resource languages like American Sign Language (Inan et al., 2022), and equitable language use (Mayfield et al., 2019).

While we still have much to learn about new generative technologies (Rogers et al., 2020), what we do know can be alarming. For example, these models typically fail to learn infrequent data concepts in the long tail of text distributions (Kandpal et al., 2022). Indeed, this can lead to unfortunate, unintended outcomes such as social inequities (Bolukbasi et al., 2016), abysmal lexical diversity (Shekhar et al., 2019), or hard to resolve toxicity issues (Xu et al., 2021). All this is to say, without doubt, our use of machine learning as a tool has outpaced our understanding of this tool in many ways. For robust, responsible deployment of generative AI, we need a principled means of analysis. This tutorial aims to meet this demand, proposing domain adaptation (DA) theory as a mechanism to study the nuanced data issues that plague our models; e.g., the linguistic and societal biases induced by long tailed data. We cover statistical tools for:

1. *training* generative models with reinforcement learning, multi-agent techniques, distillation, traditional supervision, and more;

[1] https://github.com/anthonysicilia/AACL2023-DA4GenerativeAI



*Proceedings of the 13th International Joint Conference on Natural Language Processing and the 3rd Conference of the Asia-Pacific Chapter of the Association for Computational Linguistics (Tutorial Abstracts)*, pages 14–22
November 1–4, 2023. 

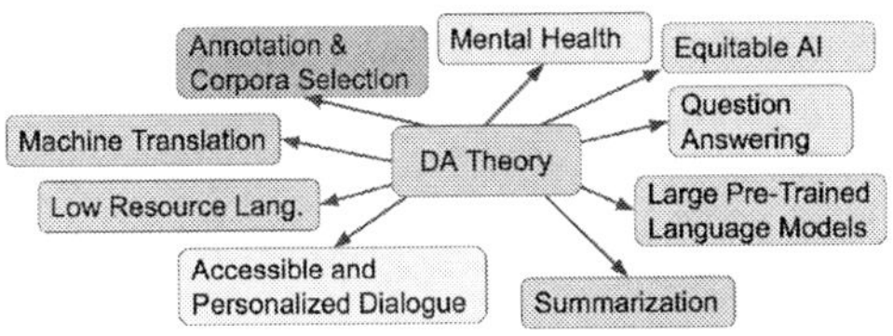


Figure 2: Overview of planned topics. Application of DA to text generation enables more than just obvious applications (e.g., model transfer). This tutorial focuses on these new emerging applications for generative AI.

2. *evaluating* the equity, human-likeness, inclusivity, and robustness of generative models;
3. and, *decision making* in small data regimes – e.g., model and dataset selection strategies.

Our accessible presentation of these tools can help to enable more robust deployment of generative AI.

While DA theory first appeared at *ACL venues over a decade ago (Blitzer et al., 2007), recently, more and more contemporary works have seen the benefit of carefully analyzing impacts of data-shift on their models. This is for good reason. DA theory allows us to answer complex questions like:

- *Will a pre-trained model generalize to my data?*
- *Can I improve generalization without much data?*
- *Is my corpus even large enough to measure bias and other language errors of a model?*

Despite its utility, the use of DA theory is not wide spread – a quick keyword search on `aclanthology` provided less than 10 papers at *ACL venues (excluding our own), which employ DA theory[2] or related techniques. This tutorial aims to bring awareness to emerging applications of DA theory to equitable, inclusive, and robust generation in an accessible way – connecting DA to more contemporary works whenever applicable.

## 2 Overview of Topics

We give a presentation plan next. For most topics, we highlight application areas or detailed questions we aim to address (see: ⋆ and italicized text), and also provide potential reading lists (see: 📑).

1. **Inclusive Generation: Setup and Motivation**
   - Language Models and Data Sources
     ⋆ *Which end-users are left behind?*
     📑 Brown et al. (2020)
   - Example: Summarizing Medical Records
     ⋆ *Are domains with limited data impacted?*
     📑 Phan et al. (2023)
   - Example: Personalized Education
     ⋆ *Can we personalize generative models for individualized student experiences?*
     📑 Hu et al. (2008)
   - Example: Assistive Legal Technologies
     ⋆ *Can generative models be robust to specification (e.g., locality) in legal applications?*
     📑 Abdallah et al. (2023)
   - Example: Inclusive and Accessible Dialogue
     ⋆ *Can generative models support users with different preferences and capabilities?*
     📑 Sicilia et al. (2023); Inan et al. (2022)
2. **Domain Adaptation Theory: The Basics**
   - Learning Theory and Adaptation Bounds
     📑 Redko et al. (2020)
   - Classifier-based Statistical Distances
     📑 Ben-David et al. (2010); Sicilia et al. (2022a);
   - Measuring Model Data-Efficiency
     📑 Shalev-Shwartz and Ben-David (2014); Sicilia et al. (2021c)
   - Domain Adaptation for Generative Models
     📑 Sicilia and Alikhani (2022)
3. **Inclusive Text-Generation Algorithms**
   - Adversarial Training for Domain Alignment
     ⋆ *Application Areas: Unsupervised and Semi-supervised Summarization*
     📑 Ganin et al. (2016); Chen and Chen (2019)
   - Other Ways to Align: Semantics and Tokens
     ⋆ *Application Areas: Out-of-Domain Machine Translation and Low Resource Languages*
     📑 Štefánik et al. (2023); Phan et al. (2023)
   - Adapters and Adapter Soups
     ⋆ *Application Area: Adapting Language Models to New Domains without Training*
     📑 Chronopoulou et al. (2022, 2023)
   - Augmentation with Generative Models
     ⋆ *Applications: Semi-supervised Question-Answering, Accessible Dialogue, Counseling*
     📑 Yang et al. (2017); Parthasarathi et al. (2020); Shen et al. (2020); Inan et al. (2022)
   - Instance Weighting for Generative AI
     ⋆ *Applications: Out-of-Domain Machine Translation and Personalized Dialogue*
     📑 Wang et al. (2017); Welch et al. (2022)
   - Domain Adaptive MLM Objectives
     ⋆ *Applications: Mental Health Risk Prediction and other Healthcare Tasks*
     📑 Aragon et al. (2023); Lu et al. (2023)

[2]We distinguish between more common DA applications, and theoretical foundations; e.g., as in Redko et al. (2020).

4. **Computational Techniques (Activity)**
   - Confidence intervals and significance
     ⋆ *Is my test set large enough?*
     Ⓡ Shalev-Shwartz and Ben-David (2014)
   - Uncertainty and Confidence for Fairness
     ⋆ *Is my model fair to protected demographics? Do I even have enough data to determine this?*
     Ⓡ Ethayarajh (2020)
   - Transferring Models across Text-Genres
     ⋆ *How can I pick datasets when transferring models to small data regimes like medicine?*
     Ⓡ Blitzer et al. (2007); Atwell et al. (2022)
   - Supplementing Expertise with Bronze labels
     ⋆ *What's the best annotation protocol when (domain expert) gold labels are too expensive?*
     Ⓡ Hao and Paul (2019); Elsahar and Gallé (2019); He et al. (2021)
5. **Equitable Text-Generation**
   - Bias, Representational Harm, & Task Success
     Ⓡ Mayfield et al. (2019); Harrington and Egede (2023)
   - Defining Bias and Equity in Text-Generation
     Ⓡ Hendricks et al. (2018); Das and Balke (2022); Sicilia and Alikhani (2023)
   - Representation Learning and Bias Projection
     ⋆ *Applications: Mitigating Social Bias in Text Embedding and Masked Language Modeling*
     Ⓡ Vargas and Cotterell (2020); Yu et al. (2023); Kumar et al. (2023)
   - Data Augmentation and Interventions
     ⋆ *Applications: Toxicity Reduction in Masked Language Models and Equitable Distillation*
     Ⓡ Sun et al. (2019); Thakur et al. (2023)
   - Reinforcement Learning and Self-Play
     ⋆ *Applications: Morality, Toxicity, and Bias in Language Models; Bias in Dialogue Systems*
     Ⓡ Liu et al. (2022); Madanagopal and Caverlee (2023); Sicilia and Alikhani (2023)
6. **Future Work**: *TBA, Time Permitting*

## 3 Tutorial Type and Length

This tutorial is meant to be a **cutting-edge** tutorial and is meant to fill up a **3 hour time slot**.

**Cutting Edge** While DA theory has been well studied in ML theory communities, practical application for inclusivity, equity, and robustness of generative AI is an emerging area. Indeed, most of the reading-list has been published in *ACL venues across the last few years. While similar areas have been discussed in past tutorials (e.g., transfer learning and learning with limited data), the focus of this tutorial is on more rigorous theoretical aspects of DA and how these techniques can be applied in the, perhaps, unexpected area of equitable and inclusive generation. Our tutorial will also pay particular attention to large language models.

**Timing** We anticipate each of the 6 numbered top-level sections will take roughly 20 minutes, leaving extra time for questions and longer sections. Every 2 sections can be followed by a break.

## 4 Prerequisite Knowledge

Some familiarity with text-generation techniques and related tasks is recommended. The tutorial content will be accessible to Senior undergraduate, masters, and PhD students. In particular, **we assume no attendee will have experience with DA theory**, and plan to explain adaptation bounds and their distribution distances in an accessible way, giving preference to visualizations and high-level descriptions (over detailed equations). If desired, attendees can expound these topics themselves after the tutorial, using **take-home resources** provided during the talk or on the tutorial website (e.g., python packages, papers, surveys, etc.).[3]

## 5 Related Tutorials

No tutorial on DA theory for inclusive and equitable generation has been provided at an *ACL venue. With that said, recent tutorials have related motivation and complementary coverage.

Dyer et al. (2016); Church et al. (2022) and multiple other tutorials have previously considered deep neural networks for NLP. Deep networks have become a dominating trend and, as noted, their complexity poses issues for confident, responsible decision making as it pertains to training and deploying these models for generative applications. Our tutorial complements these existing tutorials, and pays careful attention to tools from DA theory specifically designed for large language models (Sicilia et al., 2022a). Our hope is to make application of these models more robust.

Chien (2019) present a tutorial on Deep Bayesian techniques, Ruder et al. (2019) present a tutorial on transfer learning, Yang et al. (2022) present a tutorial on learning with limited data, and

[3] https://github.com/anthonysicilia/AACL2023-DA4GenerativeAI

Fisch et al. (2022) present a tutorial on uncertainty estimation. These tutorials set the stage for our proposed tutorial, since DA theory provides rigorous solutions to many of the problems posed within these topics. As such, we do expect some topical overlap, but all of the techniques and solutions we present to attendees are likely to be new. Attendees that were/are interested in these previous tutorials will benefit from seeing how DA theory can be applied to solve their problems in a new way.

Tripodi and Pelillo (2016) present a tutorial on game theory, Belinkov et al. (2020) present a tutorial on interpretability, and Lucic et al. (2022) present a tutorial on reproducible ML. Each of these tutorials shares a common theme with our proposed tutorial: making NLP more robust through principled analyses. Similar to these tutorials, we will provide the tools for NLP practitioners applying ML to rigorously justify their decision making processes and algorithm designs.

Finally, Chang et al. (2019) present a tutorial on bias and fairness in NLP. Our tutorial complements this previous tutorial in topic, but presents a new perspective: the application of DA theory to this area with a focus on large generative models.

## 6 Instructors

**Anthony Sicilia** is a 5th year Ph.D student, specializing in applications of learning theory and domain adaptation theory to NLP problems such as inclusivity, equity, and robustness. He has experience in practical deployment of NLP systems, leading an Alexa Prize TaskBot team (focused on inclusivity and collaboration) to 3rd place overall in this international contest. He has published 4 papers on robust NLP at *ACL venues, which are present in the reading list: Atwell et al. (2022); Sicilia and Alikhani (2022); Sicilia et al. (2022b); Sicilia and Alikhani (2023). He also received a **best paper award** at UAI 2022 for his work on novel PAC-Bayesian DA theory for multiclass neural-networks (Sicilia et al., 2022a). His work spans application of DA theory to diverse areas such as: analysis of the impact of data-shift on parsers and sentiment classifiers, dialogue management and generation in non-cooperative multi-objective environments, causal analysis of the impact of model/dataset properties on discourse analysis, human-like dialogue management and generation, equitable dialogue management and generation, evaluation of both human-likeness and equity in dialogue, and quantification of linguistic and social biases in large language models. Previously, he also applied learning theory in vision, especially small-data medical applications with a primary focus on bias mitigation and robust model evaluation (Sicilia et al., 2021a,b,c; Zhao et al., 2022).

**Malihe Alikhani** is an expert in natural language processing (NLP) and machine learning. Alikhani's research interests center on using representations of communicative structure to improve ethical and practical machine learning models. One of the main focuses of her recent research has been on studying formal methods of machine learning for designing equitable and robust NLP tasks. This includes using tools from learning theory for efficient dialogue management, text generation, classification and measuring and mitigating biases in generation and classification tasks (Atwell et al., 2022; Sicilia and Alikhani, 2022; Sicilia et al., 2022b; Atwell et al., 2021; Sicilia and Alikhani, 2023; Sicilia et al., 2022a). Her work in these areas have received three best paper awards at UAI 2022, ACM UMAP 2022 and INLG 2021.

She has designed several task-oriented dialogue systems and conversational QA models (Khalid et al., 2020b,a; Sicilia et al., 2022b). Her work has explored data-driven modeling of inferential links in text and imagery (Alikhani and Stone, 2019), neural controllable description generation models for images (Alikhani et al., 2020b), datasets and models of coherent diagram interpretation (Alikhani and Stone, 2018; Hiippala et al., 2021) and interpretation of multimodal pointing actions in human-robot collaboration (Alikhani et al., 2020a). She has worked on distributional semantic approaches for modeling lexical aspect of verbs in English and six other languages (Kober et al., 2020). She has also been involved in various projects for studying the cognitive science of language use (Persaud et al., 2017) and formal language and automata, including probabilistic models of success runs in Markov independent trials (Alikhani et al., 2015). Alikhani has collected several corpora annotated by crowdworkers and expert linguists in the area of discourse, multimodality, dialogue, human–robot interaction and psycholinguistics (Alikhani and Stone, 2019; Hiippala et al., 2021; Alikhani and Stone, 2018; Alikhani et al., 2019a, 2020a). She has designed software for annotation, formal and ML models for studying communicative intents and the context of human-machine communication (Alikhani et al., 2019b; Khalid et al., 2020b).

## References


Abdelrahman Abdallah, Bhawna Piryani, and Adam Jatowt. 2023. Exploring the state of the art in legal qa systems. *arXiv preprint arXiv:2304.06623*.

Malihe Alikhani, Sreyasi Nag Chowdhury, Gerard de Melo, and Matthew Stone. 2019a. CITE: A corpus of image-text discourse relations. In *Proceedings of the 2019 Conference of the North American Chapter of the Association for Computational Linguistics: Human Language Technologies, Volume 1 (Long and Short Papers)*, pages 570–575.

Malihe Alikhani, Baber Khalid, Rahul Shome, Chaitanya Mitash, Kostas Bekris, and Matthew Stone. 2020a. That and there: Judging the intent of pointing actions with robotic arms. 34(06):10343–10351.

Malihe Alikhani, Bjørn Kjos-Hanssen, Amirarsalan Pakravan, and Babak Saadat. 2015. Pricing complexity options. *Algorithmic Finance*, 4(3-4):127–137.

Malihe Alikhani, Ethan Selfridge, Matthew Stone, and Michael Johnston. 2019b. Multimodal decisions for conversational ai. In *Submission*.

Malihe Alikhani, Piyush Sharma, Shengjie Li, Radu Soricut, and Matthew Stone. 2020b. CLUE: Cross-modal coherence modeling for caption generation. In *Proceedings of the 58th Annual Meeting of the Association for Computational Linguistics*, pages 6525–6535.

Malihe Alikhani and Matthew Stone. 2018. Arrows are the verbs of diagrams. In *Proceedings of the 27th International Conference on Computational Linguistics*, pages 3552–3563.

Malihe Alikhani and Matthew Stone. 2019. "Caption" as a coherence relation: Evidence and implications. In *Second Workshop on Shortcomings in Vision and Language (SiVL)*.

Mario Aragon, Adrián Pastor López Monroy, Luis Gonzalez, David E Losada, and Manuel Montes. 2023. Disorbert: A double domain adaptation model for detecting signs of mental disorders in social media. In *Proceedings of the 61st Annual Meeting of the Association for Computational Linguistics (Volume 1: Long Papers)*, pages 15305–15318.

Katherine Atwell, Junyi Jessy Li, and Malihe Alikhani. 2021. Where are we in discourse relation recognition? In *Proceedings of the 22nd Annual Meeting of the Special Interest Group on Discourse and Dialogue*, pages 314–325, Singapore and Online. Association for Computational Linguistics.

Katherine Atwell, Anthony Sicilia, Seong Jae Hwang, and Malihe Alikhani. 2022. The change that matters in discourse parsing: Estimating the impact of domain shift on parser error. In *Findings of the Association for Computational Linguistics: ACL 2022*, pages 824–845, Dublin, Ireland. Association for Computational Linguistics.

Yonatan Belinkov, Sebastian Gehrmann, and Ellie Pavlick. 2020. Interpretability and analysis in neural NLP. In *Proceedings of the 58th Annual Meeting of the Association for Computational Linguistics: Tutorial Abstracts*, pages 1–5, Online. Association for Computational Linguistics.

Shai Ben-David, John Blitzer, Koby Crammer, Alex Kulesza, Fernando Pereira, and Jennifer Wortman Vaughan. 2010. A theory of learning from different domains. *Machine learning*, 79(1):151–175.

John Blitzer, Mark Dredze, and Fernando Pereira. 2007. Biographies, Bollywood, boom-boxes and blenders: Domain adaptation for sentiment classification. In *Proceedings of the 45th Annual Meeting of the Association of Computational Linguistics*, pages 440–447, Prague, Czech Republic. Association for Computational Linguistics.

Tolga Bolukbasi, Kai-Wei Chang, James Y Zou, Venkatesh Saligrama, and Adam T Kalai. 2016. Man is to computer programmer as woman is to homemaker? debiasing word embeddings. *Advances in neural information processing systems*, 29.

Tom Brown, Benjamin Mann, Nick Ryder, Melanie Subbiah, Jared D Kaplan, Prafulla Dhariwal, Arvind Neelakantan, Pranav Shyam, Girish Sastry, Amanda Askell, et al. 2020. Language models are few-shot learners. *Advances in neural information processing systems*, 33:1877–1901.

Ilias Chalkidis, Manos Fergadiotis, Prodromos Malakasiotis, Nikolaos Aletras, and Ion Androutsopoulos. 2020. Legal-bert: The muppets straight out of law school. In *Findings of the Association for Computational Linguistics: EMNLP 2020*, pages 2898–2904.

Kai-Wei Chang, Vinodkumar Prabhakaran, and Vicente Ordonez. 2019. Bias and fairness in natural language processing. In *Proceedings of the 2019 Conference on Empirical Methods in Natural Language Processing and the 9th International Joint Conference on Natural Language Processing (EMNLP-IJCNLP): Tutorial Abstracts*, Hong Kong, China. Association for Computational Linguistics.

Francine Chen and Yan-Ying Chen. 2019. Adversarial domain adaptation using artificial titles for abstractive title generation. In *Proceedings of the 57th Annual Meeting of the Association for Computational Linguistics*, pages 2197–2203, Florence, Italy. Association for Computational Linguistics.

Jen-Tzung Chien. 2019. Deep Bayesian natural language processing. In *Proceedings of the 57th Annual Meeting of the Association for Computational Linguistics: Tutorial Abstracts*, pages 25–30, Florence, Italy. Association for Computational Linguistics.

Alexandra Chronopoulou, Matthew Peters, and Jesse Dodge. 2022. Efficient hierarchical domain adaptation for pretrained language models. In *Proceedings of the 2022 Conference of the North American Chapter of the Association for Computational Linguistics:*

*Human Language Technologies*, pages 1336–1351, Seattle, United States. Association for Computational Linguistics.

Alexandra Chronopoulou, Matthew E Peters, Alexander Fraser, and Jesse Dodge. 2023. Adaptersoup: Weight averaging to improve generalization of pretrained language models. In *Findings of the Association for Computational Linguistics: EACL 2023*, pages 2009–2018.

Kenneth Church, Valia Kordoni, Gary Marcus, Ernest Davis, Yanjun Ma, and Zeyu Chen. 2022. A gentle introduction to deep nets and opportunities for the future. In *Proceedings of the 60th Annual Meeting of the Association for Computational Linguistics: Tutorial Abstracts*, pages 1–6, Dublin, Ireland. Association for Computational Linguistics.

Mayukh Das and Wolf Tilo Balke. 2022. Quantifying bias from decoding techniques in natural language generation. In *Proceedings of the 29th International Conference on Computational Linguistics*, pages 1311–1323, Gyeongju, Republic of Korea. International Committee on Computational Linguistics.

Chris Dyer, Yoav Goldberg, and Graham Neubig. 2016. Practical neural networks for NLP: From theory to code. In *Proceedings of the 2016 Conference on Empirical Methods in Natural Language Processing: Tutorial Abstracts*, Austin, Texas. Association for Computational Linguistics.

Hady Elsahar and Matthias Gallé. 2019. To annotate or not? predicting performance drop under domain shift. In *Proceedings of the 2019 Conference on Empirical Methods in Natural Language Processing and the 9th International Joint Conference on Natural Language Processing (EMNLP-IJCNLP)*, pages 2163–2173, Hong Kong, China. Association for Computational Linguistics.

Kawin Ethayarajh. 2020. Is your classifier actually biased? measuring fairness under uncertainty with bernstein bounds. In *Proceedings of the 58th Annual Meeting of the Association for Computational Linguistics*, pages 2914–2919, Online. Association for Computational Linguistics.

Adam Fisch, Robin Jia, and Tal Schuster. 2022. Uncertainty estimation for natural language processing. In *COLING*.

Yaroslav Ganin, Evgeniya Ustinova, Hana Ajakan, Pascal Germain, Hugo Larochelle, François Laviolette, Mario Marchand, and Victor Lempitsky. 2016. Domain-adversarial training of neural networks. *The journal of machine learning research*, 17(1):2096–2030.

Shudong Hao and Michael J. Paul. 2019. Analyzing Bayesian crosslingual transfer in topic models. In *Proceedings of the 2019 Conference of the North American Chapter of the Association for Computational Linguistics: Human Language Technologies, Volume 1 (Long and Short Papers)*, pages 1551–1565, Minneapolis, Minnesota. Association for Computational Linguistics.

Christina N Harrington and Lisa Egede. 2023. Trust, comfort and relatability: Understanding black older adults' perceptions of chatbot design for health information seeking. In *Proceedings of the 2023 CHI Conference on Human Factors in Computing Systems*, pages 1–18.

Hangfeng He, Mingyuan Zhang, Qiang Ning, and Dan Roth. 2021. Foreseeing the benefits of incidental supervision. In *Proceedings of the 2021 Conference on Empirical Methods in Natural Language Processing*, pages 1782–1800, Online and Punta Cana, Dominican Republic. Association for Computational Linguistics.

Lisa Anne Hendricks, Kaylee Burns, Kate Saenko, Trevor Darrell, and Anna Rohrbach. 2018. Women also snowboard: Overcoming bias in captioning models. In *Proceedings of the European conference on computer vision (ECCV)*, pages 771–787.

Tuomo Hiippala, Malihe Alikhani, Jonas Haverinen, Timo Kalliokoski, Evanfiya Logacheva, Serafina Orekhova, Aino Tuomainen, Matthew Stone, and John A Bateman. 2021. Ai2d-rst: A multimodal corpus of 1000 primary school science diagrams. *Language Resources and Evaluation*, 55(3):661–688.

Dawei Hu, Wei Chen, Qingtian Zeng, Tianyong Hao, Feng Min, and Liu Wenyin. 2008. Using a user-interactive qa system for personalized e-learning. *International Journal of Distance Education Technologies (IJDET)*, 6(3):1–22.

Mert Inan, Yang Zhong, Sabit Hassan, Lorna Quandt, and Malihe Alikhani. 2022. Modeling intensification for sign language generation: A computational approach. In *Findings of the Association for Computational Linguistics: ACL 2022*, pages 2897–2911, Dublin, Ireland. Association for Computational Linguistics.

Nikhil Kandpal, Haikang Deng, Adam Roberts, Eric Wallace, and Colin Raffel. 2022. Large language models struggle to learn long-tail knowledge. *arXiv preprint arXiv:2211.08411*.

Enkelejda Kasneci, Kathrin Seßler, Stefan Küchemann, Maria Bannert, Daryna Dementieva, Frank Fischer, Urs Gasser, Georg Groh, Stephan Günnemann, Eyke Hüllermeier, et al. 2023. Chatgpt for good? on opportunities and challenges of large language models for education. *Learning and Individual Differences*, 103:102274.

Baber Khalid, Malihe Alikhani, Michael Fellner, Brian McMahan, and Matthew Stone. 2020a. Discourse coherence, reference grounding and goal oriented dialogue. In *Proceedings of the 24th Workshop on the Semantics and Pragmatics of Dialogue - Full Papers*, Virtually at Brandeis, Waltham, New Jersey. SEMDIAL.

Baber Khalid, Malihe Alikhani, and Matthew Stone. 2020b. Combining cognitive modeling and reinforcement learning for clarification in dialogue. In *Proceedings of the 28th International Conference on Computational Linguistics*.

Thomas Kober, Stone Matthew Alikhani, Malihe, and Mark Steedman. 2020. Aspectuality across genre: A distributional semantics approach.

Deepak Kumar, Oleg Lesota, George Zerveas, Daniel Cohen, Carsten Eickhoff, Markus Schedl, and Navid Rekabsaz. 2023. Parameter-efficient modularised bias mitigation via AdapterFusion. In *Proceedings of the 17th Conference of the European Chapter of the Association for Computational Linguistics*, pages 2738–2751, Dubrovnik, Croatia. Association for Computational Linguistics.

Ruibo Liu, Ge Zhang, Xinyu Feng, and Soroush Vosoughi. 2022. Aligning generative language models with human values. In *Findings of the Association for Computational Linguistics: NAACL 2022*, pages 241–252, Seattle, United States. Association for Computational Linguistics.

Keming Lu, Peter Potash, Xihui Lin, Yuwen Sun, Zihan Qian, Zheng Yuan, Tristan Naumann, Tianxi Cai, and Junwei Lu. 2023. Prompt discriminative language models for domain adaptation. In *Proceedings of the 5th Clinical Natural Language Processing Workshop*, pages 247–258.

Ana Lucic, Maurits Bleeker, Samarth Bhargav, Jessica Forde, Koustuv Sinha, Jesse Dodge, Sasha Luccioni, and Robert Stojnic. 2022. Towards reproducible machine learning research in natural language processing. In *Proceedings of the 60th Annual Meeting of the Association for Computational Linguistics: Tutorial Abstracts*, pages 7–11, Dublin, Ireland. Association for Computational Linguistics.

Karthic Madanagopal and James Caverlee. 2023. Reinforced sequence training based subjective bias correction. In *Proceedings of the 17th Conference of the European Chapter of the Association for Computational Linguistics*, pages 2585–2598, Dubrovnik, Croatia. Association for Computational Linguistics.

Elijah Mayfield, Michael Madaio, Shrimai Prabhumoye, David Gerritsen, Brittany McLaughlin, Ezekiel Dixon-Román, and Alan W Black. 2019. Equity beyond bias in language technologies for education. In *Proceedings of the Fourteenth Workshop on Innovative Use of NLP for Building Educational Applications*, pages 444–460, Florence, Italy. Association for Computational Linguistics.

Prasanna Parthasarathi, Sharan Narang, and Arvind Neelakantan. 2020. On task-level dialogue composition of generative transformer model. In *Proceedings of the First Workshop on Insights from Negative Results in NLP*, pages 41–47.

Kimele Persaud, Brian McMahan, Malihe Alikhani, Kevin Pei, Pernille Hemmer, and Matthew Stone. 2017. When is likely unlikely: Investigating the variability of vagueness. In *Proceedings of the Cognitive Science Society Conference*.

Long Phan, Tai Dang, Hieu Tran, Trieu Trinh, Vy Phan, Lam Chau, and Minh-Thang Luong. 2023. Enriching biomedical knowledge for low-resource language through large-scale translation. In *Proceedings of the 17th Conference of the European Chapter of the Association for Computational Linguistics*, pages 3123–3134.

Ievgen Redko, Emilie Morvant, Amaury Habrard, Marc Sebban, and Younès Bennani. 2020. A survey on domain adaptation theory: learning bounds and theoretical guarantees. *arXiv preprint arXiv:2004.11829*.

Anna Rogers, Olga Kovaleva, and Anna Rumshisky. 2020. A primer in BERTology: What we know about how BERT works. *Transactions of the Association for Computational Linguistics*, 8:842–866.

Sebastian Ruder, Matthew E. Peters, Swabha Swayamdipta, and Thomas Wolf. 2019. Transfer learning in natural language processing. In *Proceedings of the 2019 Conference of the North American Chapter of the Association for Computational Linguistics: Tutorials*, pages 15–18, Minneapolis, Minnesota. Association for Computational Linguistics.

Shai Shalev-Shwartz and Shai Ben-David. 2014. *Understanding machine learning: From theory to algorithms*. Cambridge university press.

Ravi Shekhar, Aashish Venkatesh, Tim Baumgärtner, Elia Bruni, Barbara Plank, Raffaella Bernardi, and Raquel Fernández. 2019. Beyond task success: A closer look at jointly learning to see, ask, and GuessWhat. In *Proceedings of the 2019 Conference of the North American Chapter of the Association for Computational Linguistics: Human Language Technologies, Volume 1 (Long and Short Papers)*, pages 2578–2587, Minneapolis, Minnesota. Association for Computational Linguistics.

Siqi Shen, Charles Welch, Rada Mihalcea, and Verónica Pérez-Rosas. 2020. Counseling-style reflection generation using generative pretrained transformers with augmented context. In *Proceedings of the 21th Annual Meeting of the Special Interest Group on Discourse and Dialogue*, pages 10–20, 1st virtual meeting. Association for Computational Linguistics.

Anthony Sicilia and Malihe Alikhani. 2022. Leather: A framework for learning to generate human-like text in dialogue. In *Findings of the Association for Computational Linguistics: AACL-IJCNLP 2022*, pages 30–53.

Anthony Sicilia and Malihe Alikhani. 2023. Learning to generate equitable text in dialogue from biased training data. In *Annual Meeting of the Association for Computational Linguistics 2023*.

Anthony Sicilia, Katherine Atwell, Malihe Alikhani, and Seong Jae Hwang. 2022a. Pac-bayesian domain adaptation bounds for multiclass learners. In *The 38th Conference on Uncertainty in Artificial Intelligence*.

Anthony Sicilia, Jennifer C Gates, and Malihe Alikhani. 2023. How old is gpt?: The humbel framework for evaluating language models using human demographic dat. *arXiv preprint arXiv:2305.14195*.

Anthony Sicilia, Tristan Maidment, Pat Healy, and Malihe Alikhani. 2022b. Modeling non-cooperative dialogue: Theoretical and empirical insights. *Transactions of the Association for Computational Linguistics*, 10:1084–1102.

Anthony Sicilia, Xingchen Zhao, and Seong Jae Hwang. 2021a. Domain adversarial neural networks for domain generalization: When it works and how to improve. *arXiv preprint arXiv:2102.03924*.

Anthony Sicilia, Xingchen Zhao, Davneet S Minhas, Erin E O'Connor, Howard J Aizenstein, William E Klunk, Dana L Tudorascu, and Seong Jae Hwang. 2021b. Multi-domain learning by meta-learning: Taking optimal steps in multi-domain loss landscapes by inner-loop learning. In *2021 IEEE 18th International Symposium on Biomedical Imaging (ISBI)*, pages 650–654. IEEE.

Anthony Sicilia, Xingchen Zhao, Anastasia Sosnovskikh, and Seong Jae Hwang. 2021c. Pac bayesian performance guarantees for deep (stochastic) networks in medical imaging. In *Medical Image Computing and Computer Assisted Intervention–MICCAI 2021: 24th International Conference, Strasbourg, France, September 27–October 1, 2021, Proceedings, Part III 24*, pages 560–570. Springer.

Michal Štefánik, Marek Kadlcik, and Petr Sojka. 2023. Soft alignment objectives for robust adaptation of language generation. In *Proceedings of the 61st Annual Meeting of the Association for Computational Linguistics (Volume 1: Long Papers)*, pages 8837–8853, Toronto, Canada. Association for Computational Linguistics.

Tony Sun, Andrew Gaut, Shirlyn Tang, Yuxin Huang, Mai ElSherief, Jieyu Zhao, Diba Mirza, Elizabeth Belding, Kai-Wei Chang, and William Yang Wang. 2019. Mitigating gender bias in natural language processing: Literature review. In *Proceedings of the 57th Annual Meeting of the Association for Computational Linguistics*, pages 1630–1640, Florence, Italy. Association for Computational Linguistics.

Himanshu Thakur, Atishay Jain, Praneetha Vaddamanu, Paul Pu Liang, and Louis-Philippe Morency. 2023. Language models get a gender makeover: Mitigating gender bias with few-shot data interventions. In *Proceedings of the 61st Annual Meeting of the Association for Computational Linguistics (Volume 2: Short Papers)*, pages 340–351, Toronto, Canada. Association for Computational Linguistics.

Rocco Tripodi and Marcello Pelillo. 2016. Game theory and natural language: Origin, evolution and processing. In *Proceedings of the 54th Annual Meeting of the Association for Computational Linguistics: Tutorial Abstracts*, Berlin, Germany. Association for Computational Linguistics.

Furkan Ufuk. 2023. The role and limitations of large language models such as chatgpt in clinical settings and medical journalism. *Radiology*, 307(3):e230276.

Francisco Vargas and Ryan Cotterell. 2020. Exploring the linear subspace hypothesis in gender bias mitigation. In *Proceedings of the 2020 Conference on Empirical Methods in Natural Language Processing (EMNLP)*, pages 2902–2913, Online. Association for Computational Linguistics.

Rui Wang, Masao Utiyama, Lemao Liu, Kehai Chen, and Eiichiro Sumita. 2017. Instance weighting for neural machine translation domain adaptation. In *Proceedings of the 2017 Conference on Empirical Methods in Natural Language Processing*, pages 1482–1488, Copenhagen, Denmark. Association for Computational Linguistics.

Charles Welch, Chenxi Gu, Jonathan K. Kummerfeld, Veronica Perez-Rosas, and Rada Mihalcea. 2022. Leveraging similar users for personalized language modeling with limited data. In *Proceedings of the 60th Annual Meeting of the Association for Computational Linguistics (Volume 1: Long Papers)*, pages 1742–1752, Dublin, Ireland. Association for Computational Linguistics.

Albert Xu, Eshaan Pathak, Eric Wallace, Suchin Gururangan, Maarten Sap, and Dan Klein. 2021. Detoxifying language models risks marginalizing minority voices. In *Proceedings of the 2021 Conference of the North American Chapter of the Association for Computational Linguistics: Human Language Technologies*, pages 2390–2397, Online. Association for Computational Linguistics.

Diyi Yang, Ankur Parikh, and Colin Raffel. 2022. Learning with limited text data. In *Proceedings of the 60th Annual Meeting of the Association for Computational Linguistics: Tutorial Abstracts*, pages 28–31, Dublin, Ireland. Association for Computational Linguistics.

Zhilin Yang, Junjie Hu, Ruslan Salakhutdinov, and William Cohen. 2017. Semi-supervised QA with generative domain-adaptive nets. In *Proceedings of the 55th Annual Meeting of the Association for Computational Linguistics (Volume 1: Long Papers)*, pages 1040–1050, Vancouver, Canada. Association for Computational Linguistics.

Charles Yu, Sullam Jeoung, Anish Kasi, Pengfei Yu, and Heng Ji. 2023. Unlearning bias in language models by partitioning gradients. In *Findings of the Association for Computational Linguistics: ACL 2023*, pages 6032–6048.

Xingchen Zhao, Chang Liu, Anthony Sicilia, Seong Jae Hwang, and Yun Fu. 2022. Test-time fourier style calibration for domain generalization. *arXiv preprint arXiv:2205.06427*.

# Editing Large Language Models

**Ningyu Zhang**[♣], **Yunzhi Yao**[♣], **Shumin Deng**[♠]
[♣]Zhejiang University, China [♠]National University of Singapore, Singapore
{zhangningyu,yyztodd}@zju.edu.cn, shumin@nus.edu.sg
https://github.com/zjunlp/KnowledgeEditingPapers

## Abstract

Even with their impressive abilities, Large Language Models (LLMs) such as ChatGPT are not immune to issues of factual or logically consistent. Concretely, the key concern is how to seamlessly update those LLMs to correct mistakes without resorting to an exhaustive retraining or continuous training procedure, both of which can demand significant computational resources and time. Thus, the capability to edit LLMs offers an efficient solution to alter a model's behavior, notably within a distinct area of interest, without negatively impacting its performance on other tasks. Through this tutorial, we strive to acquaint interested NLP researchers with recent and emerging techniques for editing LLMs. Specifically, we aim to present a systematic and current overview of cutting-edge methods, supplemented with practical tools, and unveil new research opportunities for our audiences. All the valuable resources can be accessed at https://github.com/zjunlp/KnowledgeEditingPapers.

## 1 Introduction

**Motivation:** Large Language Models (LLMs) have showcased their immense potential in generating human-like text as demonstrated by numerous studies (Brown et al., 2020; OpenAI, 2023; Chen et al., 2022; Qiao et al., 2023; Zhao et al., 2023; Ma et al., 2023). Despite their remarkable capabilities, LLMs such as ChatGPT can sometimes falter in terms of factuality or logical consistency. They might inadvertently generate content that is harmful or offensive, and they are unaware of events that have occurred post their training phase. The challenge at hand, quite intuitively, remains how to effectively update these LLMs or rectify their errors without resorting to a complete retraining or continuous training process, both of which can be significantly resource-intensive and time-consuming. To this end, the notion of **model editing** has been proposed (Sinitsin et al., 2020; De Cao et al., 2021) which provide an efficient way to modify a model's behavior, particularly within a specified domain of interest, without compromising its performance on other inputs.

Recently, editing LLMs has garnered substantial attention due to its impressive capability to rectify errors, adapt to diverse scenarios, or customize to fulfill particular use cases. In this tutorial, we aim to offer a holistic view on the process of editing LLMs. We will explore common challenges and discuss potential solutions associated with various methodologies. Our exploration will encompass strategies for preserving LLMs' parameters and techniques for modifying them. Additionally, we will introduce a range of open-sourced tools designed for specific applications, thus providing a more comprehensive understanding of the field and its practical aspects.

Note that our tutorial is related to understanding the principles that govern how pre-trained language models encapsulate knowledge (Geva et al., 2021, 2022; Haviv et al., 2023; Hao et al., 2021; Hernandez et al., 2023; Yao et al., 2023a; Cao et al., 2023). Techniques of model editing, which involve the manipulation of external knowledge, bear similarities to knowledge augmentation approaches, since updating a model's knowledge can also be viewed as infusing new knowledge into the model. Moreover, model editing can be interpreted as a specific instance of lifelong learning (Biesialska et al., 2020) and unlearning (Wu et al., 2022; Tarun et al., 2021), wherein the model is capable of adaptively and continuously incorporating and adjusting new knowledge, while simultaneously discarding outdated and incorrect information. Furthermore, model editing could help mitigate the production of toxic or harmful language by LLMs, indicating that such techniques could be instrumental in addressing the security and privacy concerns associated with these models (Geva et al., 2022). We plan



*Proceedings of the 13th International Joint Conference on Natural Language Processing and the 3rd Conference of the Asia-Pacific Chapter of the Association for Computational Linguistics (Tutorial Abstracts)*, pages 23–28

to delve into these aspects and propose potential future directions in this area.

**Tutorial Content:** We will initiate this tutorial by defining the tasks involved in editing LLMs, and introducing evaluation metrics and benchmark datasets. Subsequently, we will provide an overview of various model editing methodologies. Initially, our focus will be on methods that preserve the parameters of LLMs. These methods operate by manipulating the model's output for specific cases through the integration of an auxiliary network with the original, unaltered model. We will then transition to methods that modify the parameters of LLMs, which aim to alter the model parameters responsible for undesirable output. Throughout the tutorial, we aim to share insights gleaned from the diverse communities engaged in LLM editing research and introduce open-sourced plug-and-play model editing toolkits. Further, we will delve into potential issues as well as opportunities associated with editing LLMs, with the goal of imparting valuable insights to the NLP community. The schedule and content outline of the tutorial can be found in Table 1 and Section 3. All tutorial slides will be available at `https://github.com/zjunlp/KnowledgeEditingPapers`.

**Relevance to AACL:** LLMs, such as ChatGPT, have significantly enriched a wide array of crucial NLP tasks, thereby commanding substantial influence across the entire community. A 2022 ACL tutorial, "Zero- and Few-Shot NLP with Pretrained Language Models" (Beltagy et al., 2022), introduces recent advancements and emerging techniques in zero- and few-shot settings based on pretrained language models. More recently, another ACL tutorial titled "Everything You Need to Know about Multilingual LLMs: Towards Fair, Performant, and Reliable Models for Languages of the World" provides an overview of Multilingual LLMs with a focus on fairness, performance, and reliability. However, currently, there is no tutorial specifically dedicated to editing LLMs. Our aim is to deliver this tutorial at AACL, where we will focus on a specific, pertinent problem for LLMs, and present an in-depth exploration of the latest work within the span of a concise 3-hour session.

## 2 Type of this Tutorial

This tutorial will encompass **cutting-edge** methodologies pertaining to the editing of LLMs. However, our content will also include **introductory material** on LLMs, designed to cater to a broad audience within the NLP community. Additionally, we plan to introduce pertinent tools beneficial for both beginners and developers in the field.

## 3 Outline

The tutorial mainly includes the following parts.

### 3.1 Introduction and Background

This part consists of: (1) Background and definition: background of editing LLMs with problem definition; (2) Metrics and datasets: a brief introduction of metrics and benchmark datasets; (3) Editing LLMs as phenomenon: the importance and impact of editing LLMs to other broader AI and NLP tasks with challenges and opportunities.

### 3.2 Methods for Preserve LLMs' Parameters

This part includes cutting-edge methods for editing LLMs with methods for preserve LLMs' parameters, including: (1) SERAC (Mitchell et al., 2022b); (2) CaliNet (Dong et al., 2022); (3) T-Patcher (Huang et al., 2023).

### 3.3 Methods for Modify LLMs' Parameters

This part includes cutting-edge methods for editing LLMs with methods for modify LLMs' parameters, including: (1) KE (De Cao et al., 2021); (2) MEND (Mitchell et al., 2022a); (3) KN (Dai et al., 2022); (4) ROME (Meng et al., 2022); (5) MEMIT (Meng et al., 2023);

### 3.4 Open-sourced Tools

This part includes the open-sourced tools *EasyEdit*[1] (Wang et al., 2023) which is an easy-to-use framework to edit LLMs. We will introduce how to use and develop model editing methods with *EasyEdit* via examples.

### 3.5 Discussion on Main Issues & Opportunities

This section will present the primary challenges and opportunities, including: (1) Generalization issues such as those encountered while performing edits in language models through multi-hop questions (Zhong et al., 2023); (2) Challenges related to locality, robustness, and safety in the context of model editing (Hoelscher-Obermaier et al., 2023); (3) Other types of model (knowledge) editing, touching on aspects such as commonsense

[1] `https://github.com/zjunlp/EasyEdit`

| Presentation Topic | Presenter | Time |
|---|---|---|
| Introduction and Background | Ningyu Zhang | 20min |
| Methods for Preserve LLMs' Parameters | Shumin Deng | 40min |
| Methods for Modify LLMs' Parameters (I) | Yunzhi Yao | 30min |
| Coffee break | - | 30min |
| Methods for Modify LLMs' Parameters (II) | Yunzhi Yao | 30min |
| Open-sourced Tools | Yunzhi Yao | 30min |
| Discussion on Main Issues & Opportunities | Ningyu Zhang | 30min |

Table 1: Tutorial Schedule

reasoning and multimodal LLMs (Gupta et al., 2023); (4) Efficient model editing using parameter-efficient tuning strategies; (5) In-context model editing approaches (Zheng et al., 2023).

## 4 Prerequisites

This tutorial is accessible to anyone with a foundational knowledge in natural language processing. In addition, a rudimentary understanding of neural networks is beneficial, and familiarity with large language models, along with parameter-efficient tuning, would be particularly advantageous.

## 5 Reading list

- "Editing Large Language Models: Problems, Methods, and Opportunities", (Yao et al., 2023b)
- "Memory-Based Model Editing at Scale", (Mitchell et al., 2022b)
- "Calibrating Factual Knowledge in Pretrained Language Models", (Dong et al., 2022)
- "Transformer-Patcher: One Mistake worth One Neuron", (Huang et al., 2023)
- "Can We Edit Factual Knowledge by In-Context Learning?", (Zheng et al., 2023)
- "Editing Factual Knowledge in Language Models", (De Cao et al., 2021)
- "Fast Model Editing at Scale", (Mitchell et al., 2022a)
- "Knowledge Neurons in Pretrained Transformers", (Dai et al., 2022)
- "Locating and Editing Factual Associations in GPT", (Meng et al., 2022)
- "Mass-Editing Memory in a Transformer", (Meng et al., 2023)
- "MQUAKE: Assessing Knowledge Editing in-Language Models via Multi-Hop Questions", (Zhong et al., 2023)
- "Can LMs Learn New Entities from Descriptions? Challenges in Propagating Injected Knowledge", (Gupta et al., 2023)
- "Detecting Edit Failures In Large Language Models: An Improved Specificity Benchmark", (Hoelscher-Obermaier et al., 2023)
- "Editing Commonsense Knowledge in GPT", (Gupta et al., 2023)

## 6 Presenters

**Ningyu Zhang** is an associate professor/doctoral supervisor at Zhejiang University, leading the group about KG and NLP technologies. He has supervised to construct a information extraction toolkit named DeepKE[2] (1.9K+ stars on Github). His research interest include knowledge graph and natural language processing. He has published many papers in top international academic conferences and journals such as Natural Machine Intelligence, Nature Communications, NeurIPS, ICLR, AAAI, IJCAI, WWW, KDD, SIGIR, ACL, ENNLP, NAACL, and IEEE/ACM Transactions on Audio Speech and Language. He has served as Area Chair for ACL 2023, ARR Action Editor, Senior Program Committee member for IJCAI 2023, Program Committee member for EMNLP, NAACL, NeurIPS, ICLR, ICML, WWW, SIGIR, KDD, AAAI, and reviewer for TKDE, TKDD. He has contributed the following tutorials:

[2] https://github.com/zjunlp/DeepKE.

(1) **IJCAI 2023 Tutorial: Open-Environment Knowledge Graph Construction and Reasoning: Challenges, Approaches, and Opportunities (3-hour tutorial)**;

(2) **AACL 2022 Tutorial: Efficient and Robust Knowledge Graph Construction (3-hour tutorial)**;

(3) **China Conference on Knowledge Graph and Semantic Computing (CCKS 2022) Tutorial: Efficient Knowledge Graph Construction and Reasoning (1.5-hour tutorial)**;

(4) **The 18th Reasoning Web Summer School: Cross-Modal Knowledge Discovery, Inference, and Challenges (3-hour tutorial)**;

(5) **Knowledge Graph Conference (KGC2023 Speakers): Efficient Knowledge Graph Construction with Pre-trained Language Models (to present)**;

Email: zhangningyu@zju.edu.cn

Homepage: `https://person.zju.edu.cn/en/ningyu`

**Yunzhi Yao** is a Ph.D candidate at at School of Computer Science and Technology, Zhejiang University. Her research interests focus on Editing Large Language Models and Knowledge-enhanced Natural Language Processing. He has been research intern at Microsoft Research Asia supervised by Shaohan Huang, and research intern at Alibaba Group. He has published many papers in ACL, EMNLP, NAACL, SIGIR. For tutorial experience, he has given talks at AI-TIME to deliver his recent works. Moreover, he is the first author of the paper "**Editing Large Language Models: Problems, Methods, and Opportunities**" which is related to this tutorial.

Email: yyztodd@zju.edu.cn

Homepage: `https://scholar.google.ch/citations?user=nAagIwEAAAAJ`

**Shumin Deng** is a research fellow at Department of Computer Science, School of Computing (SoC), National University of Singapore. She have obtained her Ph.D. degree at School of Computer Science and Technology, Zhejiang University. Her research interests focus on Natural Language Processing, Knowledge Graph, Information Extraction, Neuro-Symbolic Reasoning and LLM Reasoning. She has been awarded 2022 Outstanding Graduate of Zhejiang Province, China; 2020 Outstanding Intern in Academic Cooperation of Alibaba Group. She is a member of ACL, and a member of the Youth Working Committee of the Chinese Information Processing Society of China. She has serves as a Research Session (Information Extraction) Chair for EMNLP 2022, and a Publication Chair for CoNLL 2023. She has been a Journal Reviewer for many high-quality journals, such as TASLP, TALLIP, WWWJ, ESWA, KBS and so on; and serves as a Program Committee member for NeurIPS, ICLR, ACL, EMNLP, EACL, AACL, WWW, AAAI, IJCAI and so on. She has constructed a billion-scale Open Business Knowledge Graph (OpenBG) (Deng et al., 2023), and released a leaderboard[3] which has attracted thousands of teams and researchers. She has contributed the following tutorial:

**IJCAI 2023 Tutorial: Open-Environment Knowledge Graph Construction and Reasoning: Challenges, Approaches, and Opportunities (3-hour tutorial)**

Email: shumin@nus.edu.sg

Homepage: `https://231sm.github.io/`

## References


Iz Beltagy, Arman Cohan, Robert L. Logan IV, Sewon Min, and Sameer Singh. 2022. Zero- and few-shot NLP with pretrained language models. In *Proceedings of the 60th Annual Meeting of the Association for Computational Linguistics, ACL 2022 - Tutorial Abstracts, Dublin, Ireland, May 22-27, 2022*, pages 32–37. Association for Computational Linguistics.

Magdalena Biesialska, Katarzyna Biesialska, and Marta R. Costa-jussà. 2020. Continual lifelong learning in natural language processing: A survey. In *COLING*, pages 6523–6541. International Committee on Computational Linguistics.

Tom B. Brown, Benjamin Mann, Nick Ryder, Melanie Subbiah, Jared Kaplan, Prafulla Dhariwal, Arvind Neelakantan, Pranav Shyam, Girish Sastry, Amanda Askell, Sandhini Agarwal, Ariel Herbert-Voss, Gretchen Krueger, Tom Henighan, Rewon Child, Aditya Ramesh, Daniel M. Ziegler, Jeffrey Wu, Clemens Winter, Christopher Hesse, Mark Chen, Eric Sigler, Mateusz Litwin, Scott Gray, Benjamin Chess, Jack Clark, Christopher Berner, Sam McCandlish, Alec Radford, Ilya Sutskever, and Dario Amodei. 2020. Language models are few-shot learners. In *NeurIPS*.

Boxi Cao, Qiaoyu Tang, Hongyu Lin, Xianpei Han, Jiawei Chen, Tianshu Wang, and Le Sun. 2023. Retentive or forgetful? diving into the knowledge memorizing mechanism of language models. *arXiv preprint arXiv:2305.09144*.


[3] `https://tianchi.aliyun.com/dataset/dataDetail?dataId=122271&lang=en-us`.

Xiang Chen, Ningyu Zhang, Xin Xie, Shumin Deng, Yunzhi Yao, Chuanqi Tan, Fei Huang, Luo Si, and Huajun Chen. 2022. Knowprompt: Knowledge-aware prompt-tuning with synergistic optimization for relation extraction. In *WWW '22: The ACM Web Conference 2022, Virtual Event, Lyon, France, April 25 - 29, 2022*, pages 2778–2788. ACM.

Damai Dai, Li Dong, Yaru Hao, Zhifang Sui, Baobao Chang, and Furu Wei. 2022. Knowledge neurons in pretrained transformers. In *Proceedings of the 60th Annual Meeting of the Association for Computational Linguistics (Volume 1: Long Papers)*, pages 8493–8502, Dublin, Ireland. Association for Computational Linguistics.

Nicola De Cao, Wilker Aziz, and Ivan Titov. 2021. Editing factual knowledge in language models. In *Proceedings of the 2021 Conference on Empirical Methods in Natural Language Processing*, pages 6491–6506, Online and Punta Cana, Dominican Republic. Association for Computational Linguistics.

Shumin Deng, Chengming Wang, Zhoubo Li, Ningyu Zhang, Zelin Dai, Hehong Chen, Feiyu Xiong, Ming Yan, Qiang Chen, Mosha Chen, Jiaoyan Chen, Jeff Z. Pan, Bryan Hooi, and Huajun Chen. 2023. Construction and applications of billion-scale pre-trained multimodal business knowledge graph. In *ICDE*. IEEE.

Qingxiu Dong, Damai Dai, Yifan Song, Jingjing Xu, Zhifang Sui, and Lei Li. 2022. Calibrating factual knowledge in pretrained language models. In *Findings of the Association for Computational Linguistics: EMNLP 2022*, pages 5937–5947, Abu Dhabi, United Arab Emirates. Association for Computational Linguistics.

Mor Geva, Avi Caciularu, Kevin Wang, and Yoav Goldberg. 2022. Transformer feed-forward layers build predictions by promoting concepts in the vocabulary space. In *Proceedings of the 2022 Conference on Empirical Methods in Natural Language Processing*, pages 30–45, Abu Dhabi, United Arab Emirates. Association for Computational Linguistics.

Mor Geva, Roei Schuster, Jonathan Berant, and Omer Levy. 2021. Transformer feed-forward layers are key-value memories. In *Proceedings of the 2021 Conference on Empirical Methods in Natural Language Processing*, pages 5484–5495, Online and Punta Cana, Dominican Republic. Association for Computational Linguistics.

Anshita Gupta, Debanjan Mondal, Akshay Krishna Sheshadri, Wenlong Zhao, Xiang Lorraine Li, Sarah Wiegreffe, and Niket Tandon. 2023. Editing commonsense knowledge in GPT. *CoRR*, abs/2305.14956.

Y. Hao, Li Dong, Furu Wei, and Ke Xu. 2021. Self-attention attribution: Interpreting information interactions inside transformer. In *Proc. of AAAI*.

Adi Haviv, Ido Cohen, Jacob Gidron, Roei Schuster, Yoav Goldberg, and Mor Geva. 2023. Understanding transformer memorization recall through idioms. In *Proceedings of the 17th Conference of the European Chapter of the Association for Computational Linguistics*, pages 248–264, Dubrovnik, Croatia. Association for Computational Linguistics.

Evan Hernandez, Belinda Z. Li, and Jacob Andreas. 2023. Measuring and manipulating knowledge representations in language models. *CoRR*, abs/2304.00740.

Jason Hoelscher-Obermaier, Julia Persson, Esben Kran, Ioannis Konstas, and Fazl Barez. 2023. Detecting edit failures in large language models: An improved specificity benchmark. *CoRR*, abs/2305.17553.

Zeyu Huang, Yikang Shen, Xiaofeng Zhang, Jie Zhou, Wenge Rong, and Zhang Xiong. 2023. Transformer-patcher: One mistake worth one neuron. In *The Eleventh International Conference on Learning Representations*.

Yuxi Ma, Chi Zhang, and Song-Chun Zhu. 2023. Brain in a vat: On missing pieces towards artificial general intelligence in large language models. *CoRR*, abs/2307.03762.

Kevin Meng, David Bau, Alex Andonian, and Yonatan Belinkov. 2022. Locating and editing factual associations in GPT. *Advances in Neural Information Processing Systems*, 36.

Kevin Meng, Arnab Sen Sharma, Alex J Andonian, Yonatan Belinkov, and David Bau. 2023. Mass-editing memory in a transformer. In *The Eleventh International Conference on Learning Representations*.

Eric Mitchell, Charles Lin, Antoine Bosselut, Chelsea Finn, and Christopher D Manning. 2022a. Fast model editing at scale. In *International Conference on Learning Representations*.

Eric Mitchell, Charles Lin, Antoine Bosselut, Christopher D. Manning, and Chelsea Finn. 2022b. Memory-based model editing at scale. In *International Conference on Machine Learning*.

OpenAI. 2023. GPT-4 technical report. *CoRR*, abs/2303.08774.

Shuofei Qiao, Yixin Ou, Ningyu Zhang, Xiang Chen, Yunzhi Yao, Shumin Deng, Chuanqi Tan, Fei Huang, and Huajun Chen. 2023. Reasoning with language model prompting: A survey. In *Proceedings of the 61st Annual Meeting of the Association for Computational Linguistics (Volume 1: Long Papers), ACL 2023, Toronto, Canada, July 9-14, 2023*, pages 5368–5393. Association for Computational Linguistics.

Anton Sinitsin, Vsevolod Plokhotnyuk, Dmitry Pyrkin, Sergei Popov, and Artem Babenko. 2020. Editable neural networks. In *International Conference on Learning Representations*.

Ayush K Tarun, Vikram S Chundawat, Murari Mandal, and Mohan S. Kankanhalli. 2021. Fast yet effective machine unlearning. *IEEE transactions on neural networks and learning systems*, PP.

Peng Wang, Ningyu Zhang, Xin Xie, Yunzhi Yao, Bozhong Tian, Mengru Wang, Zekun Xi, Siyuan Cheng, Kangwei Liu, Guozhou Zheng, and Huajun Chen. 2023. Easyedit: An easy-to-use knowledge editing framework for large language models. *CoRR*, abs/2308.07269.

Ga Wu, Masoud Hashemi, and Christopher Srinivasa. 2022. Puma: Performance unchanged model augmentation for training data removal. In *AAAI Conference on Artificial Intelligence*.

Yunzhi Yao, Peng Wang, Shengyu Mao, Chuanqi Tan, Fei Huang, Huajun Chen, and Ningyu Zhang. 2023a. Knowledge rumination for pre-trained language models. *CoRR*, abs/2305.08732.

Yunzhi Yao, Peng Wang, Bozhong Tian, Siyuan Cheng, Zhoubo Li, Shumin Deng, Huajun Chen, and Ningyu Zhang. 2023b. Editing large language models: Problems, methods, and opportunities. *CoRR*, abs/2305.13172.

Wayne Xin Zhao, Kun Zhou, Junyi Li, Tianyi Tang, Xiaolei Wang, Yupeng Hou, Yingqian Min, Beichen Zhang, Junjie Zhang, Zican Dong, Yifan Du, Chen Yang, Yushuo Chen, Zhipeng Chen, Jinhao Jiang, Ruiyang Ren, Yifan Li, Xinyu Tang, Zikang Liu, Peiyu Liu, Jian-Yun Nie, and Ji-Rong Wen. 2023. A survey of large language models. *CoRR*, abs/2303.18223.

Ce Zheng, Lei Li, Qingxiu Dong, Yixuan Fan, Zhiyong Wu, Jingjing Xu, and Baobao Chang. 2023. Can we edit factual knowledge by in-context learning? *ArXiv*.

Zexuan Zhong, Zhengxuan Wu, Christopher D. Manning, Christopher Potts, and Danqi Chen. 2023. Mquake: Assessing knowledge editing in language models via multi-hop questions. *CoRR*, abs/2305.14795.

# Learning WHO Saying WHAT to WHOM in Multi-Party Conversations

**Jia-Chen Gu[1], Zhuosheng Zhang[2], Zhen-Hua Ling[1]**
[1]University of Science and Technology of China
[2]Shanghai Jiao Tong University
{gujc,zhling}@ustc.edu.cn, zhangzs@sjtu.edu.cn

## Abstract

Multi-party conversations (MPC) are a more practical and challenging scenario involving more than two interlocutors. This research topic has drawn significant attention from both academia and industry, and it is nowadays counted as one of the most promising research areas in the field of dialogue systems. In general, MPC algorithms aim at addressing the issues of *Who* saying *What* to *Whom*, specifically, who speaks, say what, and address whom. The complicated interactions between interlocutors, between utterances, and between interlocutors and utterances develop many variant tasks of MPC worth investigation. In this tutorial, we present a comprehensive survey of recent advances in MPC. In particular, we summarize recent advances on the research of MPC modeling which is categorized by *Who* saying *What* to *Whom*. Finally, we highlight the challenges which are not yet well addressed in MPC and present future research directions.

## 1 Introduction

The development of intelligent dialogue systems that are able to engage in conversations with humans, has been one of the longest running goals in artificial intelligence (Kepuska and Bohouta, 2018; Berdasco et al., 2019; Zhou et al., 2020). Thanks to breakthroughs in sequence modeling (Sutskever et al., 2014; Vaswani et al., 2017) and pre-trained language models (PLMs) (Radford et al., 2019; Devlin et al., 2019; Lewis et al., 2020), researchers have proposed various effective models for conversations between two participants (Serban et al., 2016; Wen et al., 2017; Zhang et al., 2020). Recently, researchers have paid more attention to a more practical and challenging scenario involving more than two participants, which is well known as multi-party conversations (MPC) (Ouchi and Tsuboi, 2016; Zhang et al., 2018; Le et al., 2019; Hu et al., 2019; Kummerfeld et al., 2019; Gu et al., 2021, 2022a,b, 2023; Li and

(a) Two-party conversation (b) Multi-party conversation

Figure 1: Illustration of the two-party (one-on-one chat) and multi-party (group chat) conversation instances.

Zhao, 2023). Figure 1 presents instances of two-party and multi-party conversations, corresponding to the common scenarios of one-to-one chat and group chat respectively in daily life. Utterances in a two-party conversation are posted between two interlocutors alternately, constituting a *sequential* information flow. On the other hand, each utterance in an MPC can be spoken by anyone and address anyone else in this conversation, which constitutes a *graphical* information flow.

Modeling *Who* saying *What* to *Whom* in MPC poses unique research challenges, specifically, who speaks, say what, and address whom. All these have been revisited by researchers since the emergence of neural approaches as the dominant approach for solving MPC problems. The emergence of large language models (LLMs) (Brown et al., 2020; Ouyang et al., 2022), especially ChatGPT[1], has enabled more engaging conversations in the form of two-party conversations,

[1]https://chat.openai.com/



*Proceedings of the 13th International Joint Conference on Natural Language Processing and the 3rd Conference of the Asia-Pacific Chapter of the Association for Computational Linguistics (Tutorial Abstracts)*, pages 29–34
November 1–4, 2023. 

| Slot | Theme |
|---|---|
| *Session 1:* | |
| 14:15 – 14:20 | Tutorial presenters introduction |
| 14:20 – 14:35 | Introduce the task, history and application |
| 14:35 – 14:45 | Introduce the part of datasets |
| 14:45 – 15:05 | Introduce the part of "WHO Speaks" |
| 15:05 – 15:35 | Introduce the explicit part of "Address WHOM" |
| 15:35 – 15:45 | Q&A |
| 15:45 – 16:15 | Coffee break |
| *Session 2:* | |
| 16:15 – 16:45 | Introduce the implicit part of "Address WHOM" |
| 16:45 – 17:15 | Introduce the part of "Say WHAT" |
| 17:15 – 17:30 | Challenges and open questions |
| 17:30 – 17:35 | Conclusion |
| 17:35 – 17:45 | Q&A |

Table 1: Tutorial schedule.

i.e., a conversation between an agent and a user. However, the open questions of whether ChatGPT still shows great performance in group chat, and can be adapted to the form of MPC effectively and efficiently are worth investigation. Furthermore, whether these chat-style LLMs are capable of simulating human interactions e.g., conversation and perception, among multiple agents in a virtual environment (Park et al., 2023) remains research-worthy. This tutorial will survey the cutting-edge methods for MPC, introducing key sub-areas whose combination is needed for a successful solution, which have not been covered in any previous AI & NLP conference tutorial.

## 2 Tutorial Outline

This will be a **three-hour** tutorial devoted to the **cutting-edge** topic of MPC. This tutorial will include two sessions. Each session will be 1.5h, followed by 10 minutes for Q&A and 30 minutes for a break. Each part includes an overview of the corresponding topic, widely used methods and a deep dive into representative research. The detailed tutorial schedule is shown in Table 1.

The complicated interactions between interlocutors and utterances develop many variant tasks of MPC worth investigation. For example, there are scenarios where multiple people may want to interact with a chatbot or one person interacts with several chatbots at the same time, as in a chat group, to coordinate among themselves and achieve a common goal. Thus, the ability to predict which agent in the conversation is the most likely to speak next, and conversely, when an agent must wait before interacting, is important for conducting engaging and social conversations (Pinhanez et al., 2018; de Bayser et al., 2019). Furthermore, detecting who is being addressed, i.e., who the current speaker is talking to, is also non-trivial in these conversation scenarios (Ouchi and Tsuboi, 2016; Zhang et al., 2018; Le et al., 2019; Gu et al., 2021, 2023). Last but not least, only after knowing a speaker and an addressee at the current dialogue state, can the system return an appropriate response following the conversation (Hu et al., 2019; Wang et al., 2020; Gu et al., 2022a; Li and Zhao, 2023).

### 2.1 WHO Speaks

A multi-party conversation may involve the interaction between human-human, human-machine, and machine-machine. Different speakers have different characteristics, with diverse styles, emotions, and opinions. The task of *speaker segmentation*, also known as *speaker diarisation* or *speaker change detection*, aims at finding speaker changing points in a conversation. Specifically, a speaker change occurs when the current and the previous utterances are not uttered by the same speaker. Meng et al. (2017) formulate this task as a binary utterance-pair classification to judge whether the speaker changes before and after a certain decision point. Meng et al. (2018) propose another surrogate task for general speaker modeling. This task is defined by segmenting an MPC into several parts according to speakers, each segment of which comprises one or a few consecutive sentences uttered by a particular speaker. A candidate set of speakers is also given and models are required to identify the speaker of each segment. Gu et al. (2021) propose an utterance semantics-based speaker searching task where models are asked to search for a speaker in history that shares the same speaker with the expected conversation turn.

### 2.2 Address WHOM

Existing methods on detecting who is being addressed can be generally categorized into *explicit* and *implicit* ones.

**Explicit Addressee Recognition** This task *explicitly* determines the intended addressee of an utterance. Previous studies mainly focus on predicting the addressee of only the last utterance of a conversation (Ouchi and Tsuboi, 2016; Zhang et al., 2018), while recent studies pay more attention to predicting the addressees of all utterances of a conversation (Le et al., 2019; Gu et al., 2021, 2023). Le et al. (2019) propose a who-to-whom (W2W) model to recognize and complete the addressees of all utterances in a conversation to help understand the whole conversation, given an MPC where part of the addressees are unspecified. Gu et al. (2021) propose a pre-trained MPC-BERT language model for universal MPC understanding by designing self-supervised tasks, and test it on addressee recognition. Gu et al. (2023) present graph-induced fine-tuning (GIFT) which can adapt various Transformer-based LMs by designing four types of edges to integrate graph-induced signals into attention mechanisms.

**Implicit Dialogue Disentanglement** The messages from different interlocutors on different topics are heavily interwoven. Therefore, it is necessary to disentangle a whole conversation into several threads from a data stream so that each thread is about a specific topic. Basically, most of the existing methods are designed to find out which previous utterance in the history the current utterance is replying to. Thus, this task is in essence modeling addressees *implicitly*. Kummerfeld et al. (2019) create a large-scale `#Ubuntu` IRC corpus that is 16 times larger than all previously released datasets combined. Yu and Joty (2020) formalize the link prediction of disentanglement as a pointing problem following pointer networks. Each pointing operation is modeled as a multinomial distribution over the set of previous utterances. Ma et al. (2022) propose characteristic features of speaker property and reference dependency for dialogue structure.

### 2.3 Say WHAT

Generating appropriate responses in the context of MPC is challenging due to the diverse intent topic transition and information temporality. Existing methods enabling MPC systems to decide what to say can be generally categorized into *retrieval*-based and *generation*-based methods.

**Retrieval-based** The retrieval-based methods aims at selecting the best-matched response from a set of candidates, given the context of a multi-turn conversation. The key to this task is to rank the set of response candidates according to the semantic matching between the context of an MPC and a response candidate. Ouchi and Tsuboi (2016) propose jointly modeling the tasks of response selection and addressee selection to capture what is being said to whom at each time step in a context. Zhang et al. (2018) follow this framework and improve it by updating the interlocutor embeddings role-sensitively. Gu et al. (2021) propose jointly learning who says what to whom in a unified framework by considering addressee- and speaker-related tasks as complementary signals for response selection during the pre-training stage.

**Generation-based** The generation-based methods synthesize a response with generative models by maximizing its generation probability given the previous conversation history. Hu et al. (2019) propose a graph-structured neural network, the core of which is to encode utterances based on the graph topology rather than the sequence of their appearances in a conversation, to model the information flow as *graphical*. Gu et al. (2022a) propose to model complicated interactions between utterances and interlocutors with a heterogeneous graph, where two types of graph nodes and six types of edges are designed to model heterogeneity in MPC. Li and Zhao (2023) propose an EM approach that iteratively performs the expectation steps to generate missing addressees, and the maximization steps to optimize a generative model.

### 2.4 Open Challenges

**Robustness to Addressee Scarcity** Existing methods rely heavily on the necessary addressee labels and can only be applied to an ideal setting where each utterance must be tagged with an addressee label. In practice, statistics show that addressees of 55% of the utterances in the Ubuntu IRC dataset (Ouchi and Tsuboi, 2016) are not specified. Given an MPC with a few addressee labels missing, existing methods fail to build a consecutively connected conversation graph, but only a few separate conversation fragments instead. Despite Li and Zhao (2023) make preliminary exploration on the scarcity of addressee, the cost of missing addressee inference is too high, and currently only the silver label for the last utterance in a conversation is affordable to infer. A future research direction could be ensuring message passing between these conversation fragments and enhancing the robustness to addressee scarcity.

**Universal MPC Understanding** Most existing studies design models for each individual task in MPC separately. Intuitively, the complicated interactions between interlocutors and utterances might make these tasks complementary among each other. Making use of these tasks simultaneously may produce better contextualized representations of interlocutors and utterances, and would enhance the conversation understanding. Gu et al. (2021) focus on modeling only interlocutor structures and utterance semantics. A future research direction could be designing better supervised tasks for augmenting LLMs with more abilities, and being tested on more tasks to evaluate model robustness and generalization. With the rapid growth of LLMs, machine-machine interaction also becomes an important direction, where the machines may collaborate, debate, and evolve via MPC.

**Topic Transition** Despite the remarkable ability of LLMs to comprehend and generate language, the performance would drop significantly when its comes to topic transition and long context. This is precisely where a good MPC system excels. An MPC system should be able to track topic transitions and update the conversation structure dynamically as a conversation proceeds, so that it can understand deep semantics and structures of an MPC. Modeling topic transitions in MPC which tracks the specific flows of multiple ongoing sub-conversations at a fine granularity could serve as a surrogate task for complex context understanding.

## 3 Tutorial Presenters

**Jia-Chen Gu** is currently a Postdoctoral Researcher at University of Science and Technology of China. His research interests lie within machine learning for dialogue systems. Homepage: `http://home.ustc.edu.cn/~gujc/`

**Zhuosheng Zhang** is currently an Assistant Professor at Shanghai Jiao Tong University. His research interests include natural language processing, dialogue systems, and large language models. He has given a tutorial on Machine Reading Comprehension: The Role of Contextualized Language Models and Beyond at IJCAI 2021. Homepage: `https://bcmi.sjtu.edu.cn/~zhangzs/`

**Zhen-Hua Ling** is a Professor with the University of Science and Technology of China. He was a Visiting Scholar at the University of Washington and a Marie Curie Fellow at the University of Edinburgh. His research interests include speech processing and natural language processing. He was the recipient of the IEEE Signal Processing Society Young Author Best Paper Award in 2010. He was an Associate Editor of IEEE/ACM Transcations on Audio, Speech, and Language Processing from 2014 to 2018. Homepage: `http://staff.ustc.edu.cn/~zhling/`

## 4 Diversity Considerations

The MPC techniques we introduce is language agnostic. Thus, they can be applied to data in various languages and localities with some extent of adaption to scale beyond English. Presenters will share this tutorial with a worldwide audience by promoting on social media. Presenters span over junior (J.-C. Gu and Z. Zhang) and senior researchers (Z.-H. Ling). Thus, we have diversified instructors which will also help encourage diverse audience. J.-C. Gu and Z. Zhang have experience co-organizing NLP Workshops, and actively work on inviting undergraduate students to research and promoting diversity. We will work with *ACL D&I teams, and consult resources to diversify our audience participation.

## 5 Prerequisite

The prerequisite includes familiarity with basic machine learning and deep learning models, especially those typically used in modern NLP for MPC, including representation learning, Transformers, etc. Furthermore, this tutorial assumes background in basic probability, linear algebra, and calculus. We will also provide introductory materials.

**Reading List** The presenters have survey papers for comprehensive references (Gu et al., 2022b; Zhang and Zhao, 2021). The following papers are also recommended: Ouchi and Tsuboi (2016); Hu et al. (2019); Kummerfeld et al. (2019); Gu et al. (2021); Ma et al. (2022); Gu et al. (2022a); Li and Zhao (2023); Gu et al. (2023).

**Breadth** While dozens of relevant papers over the tutorial are provided, we plan to cover around 10-15 research papers in detail. Only 3-5 of the "deep dive" papers come from the presenter team.

## 6 Tutorial Details

**Audience Size** Audience sizes for physical and virtual meetings are expected to be around 100 and 150 respectively.

**Open Access** The slides, code and other teaching materials will be released online for public access. The video recording of our tutorial will also be included in the ACL Anthology.

## 7 Ethics Statement

Certain conversation data might come from private dialogues between people. Thus, privacy considerations must be taken to ensure all data that is released conforms to regulations and are under consent. As conversations and pre-trained language models may have bias in various forms, MPC models may contain the same form of bias and should be reviewed and modified if necessary.

## References


Ana Berdasco, Gustavo López, Ignacio Díaz-Oreiro, Luis Quesada, and Luis A. Guerrero. 2019. User experience comparison of intelligent personal assistants: Alexa, google assistant, siri and cortana. In *13th International Conference on Ubiquitous Computing and Ambient Intelligence, UCAmI 2019, Toledo, Spain, December 2-5, 2019*, volume 31 of *MDPI Proceedings*, page 51. MDPI.

Tom B. Brown, Benjamin Mann, Nick Ryder, Melanie Subbiah, Jared Kaplan, Prafulla Dhariwal, Arvind Neelakantan, Pranav Shyam, Girish Sastry, Amanda Askell, Sandhini Agarwal, Ariel Herbert-Voss, Gretchen Krueger, Tom Henighan, Rewon Child, Aditya Ramesh, et al. 2020. Language models are few-shot learners. In *Advances in Neural Information Processing Systems 33: Annual Conference on Neural Information Processing Systems 2020, NeurIPS 2020, December 6-12, 2020, virtual*.

Maíra Gatti de Bayser, Paulo Rodrigo Cavalin, Claudio S. Pinhanez, and Bianca Zadrozny. 2019. Learning multi-party turn-taking models from dialogue logs. *CoRR*, abs/1907.02090.

Jacob Devlin, Ming-Wei Chang, Kenton Lee, and Kristina Toutanova. 2019. BERT: pre-training of deep bidirectional transformers for language understanding. In *Proceedings of the 2019 Conference of the North American Chapter of the Association for Computational Linguistics: Human Language Technologies, NAACL-HLT 2019, Minneapolis, MN, USA, June 2-7, 2019, Volume 1 (Long and Short Papers)*, pages 4171–4186.

Jia-Chen Gu, Zhenhua Ling, Quan Liu, Cong Liu, and Guoping Hu. 2023. GIFT: graph-induced fine-tuning for multi-party conversation understanding. In *Proceedings of the 61st Annual Meeting of the Association for Computational Linguistics (Volume 1: Long Papers), ACL 2023, Toronto, Canada, July 9-14, 2023*, pages 11645–11658. Association for Computational Linguistics.

Jia-Chen Gu, Chao-Hong Tan, Chongyang Tao, Zhen-Hua Ling, Huang Hu, Xiubo Geng, and Daxin Jiang. 2022a. HeterMPC: A heterogeneous graph neural network for response generation in multi-party conversations. In *Proceedings of the 60th Annual Meeting of the Association for Computational Linguistics (Volume 1: Long Papers), ACL 2022, Dublin, Ireland, May 22-27, 2022*, pages 5086–5097. Association for Computational Linguistics.

Jia-Chen Gu, Chongyang Tao, and Zhen-Hua Ling. 2022b. Who says what to whom: A survey of multi-party conversations. In *Proceedings of the Thirty-First International Joint Conference on Artificial Intelligence, IJCAI 2022, Vienna, Austria, 23-29 July 2022*, pages 5486–5493. ijcai.org.

Jia-Chen Gu, Chongyang Tao, Zhen-Hua Ling, Can Xu, Xiubo Geng, and Daxin Jiang. 2021. MPC-BERT: A pre-trained language model for multi-party conversation understanding. In *Proceedings of the 59th Annual Meeting of the Association for Computational Linguistics and the 11th International Joint Conference on Natural Language Processing, ACL/IJCNLP 2021, (Volume 1: Long Papers), Virtual Event, August 1-6, 2021*, pages 3682–3692. Association for Computational Linguistics.

Wenpeng Hu, Zhangming Chan, Bing Liu, Dongyan Zhao, Jinwen Ma, and Rui Yan. 2019. GSN: A graph-structured network for multi-party dialogues. In *Proceedings of the Twenty-Eighth International Joint Conference on Artificial Intelligence, IJCAI 2019, Macao, China, August 10-16, 2019*, pages 5010–5016.

Veton Kepuska and Gamal Bohouta. 2018. Next-generation of virtual personal assistants (microsoft cortana, apple siri, amazon alexa and google home). In *IEEE 8th Annual Computing and Communication Workshop and Conference, CCWC 2018, Las Vegas, NV, USA, January 8-10, 2018*, pages 99–103. IEEE.

Jonathan K. Kummerfeld, Sai R. Gouravajhala, Joseph Peper, Vignesh Athreya, R. Chulaka Gunasekara, Jatin Ganhotra, Siva Sankalp Patel, Lazaros C. Polymenakos, and Walter S. Lasecki. 2019. A large-scale corpus for conversation disentanglement. In *Proceedings of the 57th Conference of the Association for Computational Linguistics, ACL 2019, Florence, Italy, July 28- August 2, 2019, Volume 1: Long Papers*, pages 3846–3856.

Ran Le, Wenpeng Hu, Mingyue Shang, Zhenjun You, Lidong Bing, Dongyan Zhao, and Rui Yan. 2019. Who is speaking to whom? learning to identify utterance addressee in multi-party conversations. In *Proceedings of the 2019 Conference on Empirical Methods in Natural Language Processing and the 9th International Joint Conference on Natural Language Processing, EMNLP-IJCNLP 2019, Hong Kong, China, November 3-7, 2019*, pages 1909–1919.

Mike Lewis, Yinhan Liu, Naman Goyal, Marjan Ghazvininejad, Abdelrahman Mohamed, Omer Levy, Veselin Stoyanov, and Luke Zettlemoyer. 2020. BART: denoising sequence-to-sequence pre-training for natural language generation, translation, and comprehension. In *Proceedings of the 58th Annual Meeting of the Association for Computational Linguistics, ACL 2020, Online, July 5-10, 2020*, pages 7871–7880. Association for Computational Linguistics.

Yiyang Li and Hai Zhao. 2023. EM pre-training for multi-party dialogue response generation. In *Proceedings of the 61st Annual Meeting of the Association for Computational Linguistics, ACL 2023, (Volume 1: Long Papers), Toronto, Canada, July 9-14, 2023*. Association for Computational Linguistics.

Xinbei Ma, Zhuosheng Zhang, and Hai Zhao. 2022. Structural characterization for dialogue disentanglement. In *Proceedings of the 60th Annual Meeting of the Association for Computational Linguistics (Volume 1: Long Papers), ACL 2022, Dublin, Ireland, May 22-27, 2022*, pages 285–297. Association for Computational Linguistics.

Zhao Meng, Lili Mou, and Zhi Jin. 2017. Hierarchical RNN with static sentence-level attention for text-based speaker change detection. In *Proceedings of the 2017 ACM on Conference on Information and Knowledge Management, CIKM 2017, Singapore, November 06 - 10, 2017*, pages 2203–2206. ACM.

Zhao Meng, Lili Mou, and Zhi Jin. 2018. Towards neural speaker modeling in multi-party conversation: The task, dataset, and models. In *Proceedings of the Eleventh International Conference on Language Resources and Evaluation, LREC 2018, Miyazaki, Japan, May 7-12, 2018*. European Language Resources Association (ELRA).

Hiroki Ouchi and Yuta Tsuboi. 2016. Addressee and response selection for multi-party conversation. In *Proceedings of the 2016 Conference on Empirical Methods in Natural Language Processing, EMNLP 2016, Austin, Texas, USA, November 1-4, 2016*, pages 2133–2143.

Long Ouyang, Jeffrey Wu, Xu Jiang, Diogo Almeida, Carroll L. Wainwright, Pamela Mishkin, Chong Zhang, Sandhini Agarwal, Katarina Slama, Alex Ray, John Schulman, Jacob Hilton, Fraser Kelton, Luke Miller, Maddie Simens, Amanda Askell, Peter Welinder, Paul F. Christiano, Jan Leike, and Ryan Lowe. 2022. Training language models to follow instructions with human feedback. In *Advances in Neural Information Processing Systems 35: Annual Conference on Neural Information Processing Systems 2022, NeurIPS 2022*.

Joon Sung Park, Joseph C. O'Brien, Carrie J. Cai, Meredith Ringel Morris, Percy Liang, and Michael S. Bernstein. 2023. Generative agents: Interactive simulacra of human behavior. *CoRR*, abs/2304.03442.

Claudio S. Pinhanez, Heloisa Candello, Mauro Carlos Pichiliani, Marisa Vasconcelos, Melina Alberio Guerra, Maíra Gatti de Bayser, and Paulo Rodrigo Cavalin. 2018. Different but equal: Comparing user collaboration with digital personal assistants vs. teams of expert agents. *CoRR*, abs/1808.08157.

Alec Radford, Jeffrey Wu, Rewon Child, David Luan, Dario Amodei, and Ilya Sutskever. 2019. Language models are unsupervised multitask learners. *OpenAI blog*, 1(8):9.

Iulian Vlad Serban, Alessandro Sordoni, Yoshua Bengio, Aaron C. Courville, and Joelle Pineau. 2016. Building end-to-end dialogue systems using generative hierarchical neural network models. In *Proceedings of the Thirtieth AAAI Conference on Artificial Intelligence, February 12-17, 2016, Phoenix, Arizona, USA*, pages 3776–3784.

Ilya Sutskever, Oriol Vinyals, and Quoc V. Le. 2014. Sequence to sequence learning with neural networks. In *Advances in Neural Information Processing Systems 27: Annual Conference on Neural Information Processing Systems 2014, December 8-13 2014, Montreal, Quebec, Canada*, pages 3104–3112.

Ashish Vaswani, Noam Shazeer, Niki Parmar, Jakob Uszkoreit, Llion Jones, Aidan N. Gomez, Lukasz Kaiser, and Illia Polosukhin. 2017. Attention is all you need. In *Advances in Neural Information Processing Systems 30: Annual Conference on Neural Information Processing Systems 2017, December 4-9, 2017, Long Beach, CA, USA*, pages 5998–6008.

Weishi Wang, Steven C. H. Hoi, and Shafiq R. Joty. 2020. Response selection for multi-party conversations with dynamic topic tracking. In *Proceedings of the 2020 Conference on Empirical Methods in Natural Language Processing, EMNLP 2020, Online, November 16-20, 2020*, pages 6581–6591.

Tsung-Hsien Wen, David Vandyke, Nikola Mrksic, Milica Gasic, Lina Maria Rojas-Barahona, Pei-Hao Su, Stefan Ultes, and Steve J. Young. 2017. A network-based end-to-end trainable task-oriented dialogue system. In *Proceedings of the 15th Conference of the European Chapter of the Association for Computational Linguistics, EACL 2017, Valencia, Spain, April 3-7, 2017, Volume 1: Long Papers*, pages 438–449.

Tao Yu and Shafiq R. Joty. 2020. Online conversation disentanglement with pointer networks. In *Proceedings of the 2020 Conference on Empirical Methods in Natural Language Processing, EMNLP 2020, Online, November 16-20, 2020*, pages 6321–6330. Association for Computational Linguistics.

Rui Zhang, Honglak Lee, Lazaros Polymenakos, and Dragomir R. Radev. 2018. Addressee and response selection in multi-party conversations with speaker interaction rnns. In *Proceedings of the Thirty-Second AAAI Conference on Artificial Intelligence, (AAAI-18), New Orleans, Louisiana, USA, February 2-7, 2018*, pages 5690–5697.

Yizhe Zhang, Siqi Sun, Michel Galley, Yen-Chun Chen, Chris Brockett, Xiang Gao, Jianfeng Gao, Jingjing Liu, and Bill Dolan. 2020. DIALOGPT : Large-scale generative pre-training for conversational response generation. In *Proceedings of the 58th Annual Meeting of the Association for Computational Linguistics: System Demonstrations, ACL 2020, Online, July 5-10, 2020*, pages 270–278. Association for Computational Linguistics.

Zhuosheng Zhang and Hai Zhao. 2021. Advances in multi-turn dialogue comprehension: A survey. *arXiv preprint arXiv:2103.03125*.

Li Zhou, Jianfeng Gao, Di Li, and Heung-Yeung Shum. 2020. The design and implementation of xiaoice, an empathetic social chatbot. *Comput. Linguistics*, 46(1):53–93.

# Developing State-Of-The-Art Massively Multilingual Machine Translation Systems for Related Languages

**Jay Gala**
AI4Bharat, IIT Madras, India
jaygala24@gmail.com

**Pranjal A. Chitale**
IIT Madras, India
cs21s022@cse.iitm.ac.in

**Raj Dabre**
National Institute of Information and Communications Technology (NICT)
Hikaridai 3-5, Seika-cho, Soraku-gun, Kyoto, Japan
raj.dabre@nict.go.jp

## Abstract

The race for developing state-of-the-art (SOTA) machine translation (MT) systems often gives the impression that this can only be done by large organizations, most of which do not fully open-source their systems. In this tutorial, we dispel this myth by generalizing our experiences in developing SOTA MT systems for related languages. We cover topics ranging from (a) the history of MT systems for related languages, (b) curating high-quality datasets, manually created as well as mined, (c) creating domain-diverse benchmarks, (d) compact but high-quality open-source MT systems that surpass other systems despite being an order of magnitude smaller in terms of parameters and computational costs than massively multilingual generic systems and (e) robust automatic and human evaluation. We hope that our tutorial encourages other groups, regardless of scale, to engage in focussed efforts on related languages or language groups to develop open-source, high-quality MT systems.

## 1 Relevance to the CL Community

With increasing access to the web, the amount of online content keeps growing rapidly, especially in developing countries which are typically multilingual. For example, India has over 1000 languages, 22 of which are spoken by over 96.71%[1] of the population. Therefore, it becomes increasingly important to develop high-quality machine translation systems catering to a variety of languages and domains. Within a country, there are often language groups containing related languages, and thus it behooves researchers to focus on models for such language groups rather than generic language agnostic systems. However, developing such systems, despite the growth in the field of MT, still remains a challenge for a vast majority of researchers. The missing link according to us is a principled answer to the following question:

***What does it take to build a SOTA massively multilingual MT system for related languages?***

Especially, answering this question will enable smaller-scale organizations to narrow their efforts and develop data and models allowing them to compete with larger organizations. We think that the CL community, which is mostly composed of such marginalized groups, will certainly benefit from our tutorial and our experiences.

## 2 Tutorial Overview

The focus of this tutorial will be an in-depth exploration of the fundamental components that constitute any massively multilingual Neural Machine Translation (NMT) system. While it might seem like building state-of-the-art (SOTA) systems can only be done by big organizations, we make the case that for related languages or language families, this need not be the case. This tutorial will draw upon our years-long experiences in developing machine translation systems for related languages, in particular, our recent work on IndicTrans2 (AI4Bharat et al., 2023).

Initially, we will begin by presenting a concise survey of the advancements made in machine translation (MT) systems, highlighting the current state of related languages, specifically Indic languages, and emphasizing the need for targeted efforts to ensure that related languages, especially low-resource languages, are not marginalized. Subsequently, we will delve into a comprehensive discussion of each of the four key building blocks:

[1] https://www.deccanherald.com/national/the-population-of-india-and-its-diversity-in-language-754286.html



*Proceedings of the 13th International Joint Conference on Natural Language Processing and the 3rd Conference of the Asia-Pacific Chapter of the Association for Computational Linguistics (Tutorial Abstracts)*, pages 35–42
November 1–4, 2023. 

"Data," "Models," "Benchmarks," and "Evaluation." Throughout these discussions, we will address several pivotal aspects, including the tradeoff between data quality and scale, the impact of high-quality human-annotated data, the benefits of script sharing for improved transfer learning between related languages, the effectiveness of data augmentation techniques, the necessity for creating benchmarks relevant to contemporary use cases, the importance of demography-specific benchmarks, the need for careful evaluation due to existing gaps in MT model assessment, and the crucial need of calibration of model-based metrics amidst the prevailing hype. By examining these essential elements, the tutorial aims to provide participants with a comprehensive understanding of the intricacies and challenges associated with developing inclusive multilingual NMT systems that are efficient and superior in performance. Such practices, when applied to a focused set of languages, especially related languages, should enable smaller groups to develop SOTA MT systems.

Throughout the tutorial, we will first start out by discussing the experiences of existing prominent works, especially for related languages, and then zoom into specific practices we found useful for IndicTrans2 as a use case.

## 3 Tutorial Outline

1. Brief introduction to Machine Translation (MT) and related languages (30 mins)
    - History of NMT (Sutskever et al., 2014; Bahdanau et al., 2015; Vaswani et al., 2017; Johnson et al., 2017; Arivazhagan et al., 2019; Aharoni et al., 2019; Bapna et al., 2022; Team et al., 2022)
    - MT architectures (RNN (Rumelhart et al., 1986; Hochreiter and Schmidhuber, 1997) / Transformer (Vaswani et al., 2017) / MoE (Fedus et al., 2022))
    - Prominent MT systems (Google Translate, Microsoft Azure Translate, M2M (Fan et al., 2020), NLLB (Team et al., 2022), IndicTrans1 (Ramesh et al., 2022), etc)
    - Make the case for language group-specific models (motivated by IndicTrans1 (Ramesh et al., 2022), IndicBART (Dabre et al., 2022), IndoBERT (Koto et al., 2020), IndoBART (Cahyawijaya et al., 2021), and other language group-specific models like AfroMT (Reid et al., 2021), CreoleM2M [2])

2. Establish the main considerations for building SOTA models (10 mins)
    - Briefly cover important aspects: data, benchmarks, modeling (size vs performance), and evaluation.
    - Touch upon what this implies for related languages (high potential of transfer learning while ensuring compactness) (Kunchukuttan and Bhattacharyya, 2020)

3. Data collection and creation (30 mins)
    - Collecting monolingual data (Conneau et al., 2020; Cahyawijaya et al., 2021; Kakwani et al., 2020; Xue et al., 2021; Doddapaneni et al., 2023; Aralikatte et al., 2023)
    - Mining parallel data (mining approaches and challenges) (El-Kishky et al., 2020; Schwenk et al., 2021; Ramesh et al., 2022; AI4Bharat et al., 2023)
    - Clean/Seed data creation (ILCI, Massive, NLLB, and IndicTrans2 efforts) (Jha, 2010; Bastianelli et al., 2020; FitzGerald et al., 2022; Team et al., 2022; AI4Bharat et al., 2023)
    - Quality vs Scale tradeoff (Bansal et al., 2022)
    - Note on scripts and writing systems

4. Focused discussion on benchmarks (20 mins)
    - Overview of existing benchmarks (Shared Task Benchmarks for Indic languages (Bojar et al., 2014; Barrault et al., 2019, 2020; Nakazawa et al., 2020, 2021), FLORES (Goyal et al., 2022; Team et al., 2022), NTREX (Federmann et al., 2022))
    - Benchmark creation Process and Quality Control (FLORES (Goyal et al., 2022; Team et al., 2022) and IN22 (AI4Bharat et al., 2023)).
    - Importance of representing domains (diversity is important)

[2] `https://huggingface.co/prajdabre/CreoleM2M`

- Importance of source-original nature of benchmarks (Zhang and Toral, 2019).

5. Break

6. Modeling (25 mins)

   - Handling vocabulary, script mapping for related languages (Sennrich et al., 2016; Kudo and Richardson, 2018; Kunchukuttan, 2020; Ramesh et al., 2022)
   - Model architectures: depth v/s width (Kong et al., 2021; Li et al., 2022)
   - Training pipelines (importance of multi-stage training) (Dabre et al., 2019; Mohiuddin et al., 2022)

7. Evaluation (40 mins)

   - Automatic evaluation and choices of metrics (BLEU (Papineni et al., 2002), chrF (Popović, 2015, 2017), COMET (Rei et al., 2020, 2022), etc.) and pros/cons.
   - Common caveats in NMT evaluation and Recommendations for Good Evaluation Practices (Post, 2018; Kocmi et al., 2021; Moghe et al., 2022; Vilar et al., 2022)
   - Observations of existing models (prominent models like NLLB, IndicTrans2, Google Translate, etc.)
   - Zero-shot performance due to language relatedness.
   - Human evaluation approaches (Adequacy/Fluency, XSTS (Agirre et al., 2016; Licht et al., 2022; Team et al., 2022), etc) and correlation with automatic metrics

8. Limitations and Future Directions (15 mins)

   - Coverage of dialects and more languages.
   - Connection with LLMs (ChatGPT,[3] BLOOM (Workshop et al., 2023))
   - Extension to speech translation

9. Summary and conclusion (10 mins)

**Total time** 180 mins

**Type of the Tutorial** Cutting-edge.

[3]https://platform.openai.com/docs/models/gpt-3-5

**Target Audience and Size** Machine translation and natural language generation (NLG) researchers and engineers. 20-40 people.

**Prerequisites** Familiarity with machine translation.

**Reading List** (Dabre et al., 2020)

**Special Requirements** N/A

**Ethical Considerations** Nothing particular except for biases in data and MT models.

## 4 Tutorial Instructors

**Jay Gala** (jaygala24@gmail.com) received his B.E. from the University of Mumbai, India. He is an AI resident at AI4Bharat, where he primarily works on building open-source models, datasets, and benchmarks for Indian languages. His research interests broadly span in the area of multimodal and multilingual representation learning, specifically in the context of data-efficient learning, training dynamics, and generalization.

**Pranjal A. Chitale** (cs21s022@cse.iitm.ac.in) received his B.E. from the University of Mumbai, India. He is currently an M.S. student at IIT Madras advised by Prof. Mitesh Khapra, working at the AI4Bharat lab. His interests lie in the fields of multilingual learning and data-efficient techniques and works on building open-source datasets, models, and benchmarks for Indic languages. His thesis work will be primarily focused on the development of multilingual NMT systems for Indian languages.

**Raj Dabre** (raj.dabre@nict.go.jp) received his M.Tech. from IIT Bombay, India and his Ph.D. from Kyoto University, Japan. He is a researcher at NICT, Japan and a visiting researcher at AI4Bharat. His research interests center on natural language processing, particularly neural machine translation for low resource languages, and on model compression and computing efficiency. He has MT and NLG related publications in ACL, EMNLP, AAAI, NAACL, COLING, INTERSPEECH and WMT. He is a current member of the organizing committee of the Workshop on Asian Translation. He has previously conducted tutorials on neural machine translation and multilingual machine translation at IJCNLP 2017 and COLING 2020, respectively.

## References


Eneko Agirre, Carmen Banea, Daniel Cer, Mona Diab, Aitor Gonzalez-Agirre, Rada Mihalcea, German Rigau, and Janyce Wiebe. 2016. SemEval-2016 task 1: Semantic textual similarity, monolingual and cross-lingual evaluation. In *Proceedings of the 10th International Workshop on Semantic Evaluation (SemEval-2016)*, pages 497–511, San Diego, California. Association for Computational Linguistics.

Roee Aharoni, Melvin Johnson, and Orhan Firat. 2019. Massively multilingual neural machine translation. In *Proceedings of the 2019 Conference of the North American Chapter of the Association for Computational Linguistics: Human Language Technologies, NAACL-HLT 2019, Minneapolis, MN, USA, June 2-7, 2019, Volume 1 (Long and Short Papers)*, pages 3874–3884. Association for Computational Linguistics.

AI4Bharat, Jay Gala, Pranjal A. Chitale, Raghavan AK, Sumanth Doddapaneni, Varun Gumma, Aswanth Kumar, Janki Nawale, Anupama Sujatha, Ratish Puduppully, Vivek Raghavan, Pratyush Kumar, Mitesh M. Khapra, Raj Dabre, and Anoop Kunchukuttan. 2023. Indictrans2: Towards high-quality and accessible machine translation models for all 22 scheduled indian languages.

Rahul Aralikatte, Ziling Cheng, Sumanth Doddapaneni, and Jackie Chi Kit Cheung. 2023. Vārta: A large-scale headline-generation dataset for indic languages.

Naveen Arivazhagan, Ankur Bapna, Orhan Firat, Roee Aharoni, Melvin Johnson, and Wolfgang Macherey. 2019. The missing ingredient in zero-shot neural machine translation. *CoRR*, abs/1903.07091.

Dzmitry Bahdanau, Kyunghyun Cho, and Yoshua Bengio. 2015. Neural machine translation by jointly learning to align and translate. In *3rd International Conference on Learning Representations, ICLR 2015, San Diego, CA, USA, May 7-9, 2015, Conference Track Proceedings*.

Yamini Bansal, B. Ghorbani, Ankush Garg, Biao Zhang, M. Krikun, Colin Cherry, Behnam Neyshabur, and Orhan Firat. 2022. Data scaling laws in nmt: The effect of noise and architecture. *International Conference On Machine Learning*.

Ankur Bapna, Isaac Caswell, Julia Kreutzer, Orhan Firat, Daan van Esch, Aditya Siddhant, Mengmeng Niu, Pallavi Baljekar, Xavier Garcia, Wolfgang Macherey, Theresa Breiner, Vera Axelrod, Jason Riesa, Yuan Cao, Mia Xu Chen, Klaus Macherey, Maxim Krikun, Pidong Wang, Alexander Gutkin, Apurva Shah, Yanping Huang, Zhifeng Chen, Yonghui Wu, and Macduff Hughes. 2022. Building machine translation systems for the next thousand languages. *CoRR*, abs/2205.03983.

Loïc Barrault, Magdalena Biesialska, Ondřej Bojar, Marta R. Costa-jussà, Christian Federmann, Yvette Graham, Roman Grundkiewicz, Barry Haddow, Matthias Huck, Eric Joanis, Tom Kocmi, Philipp Koehn, Chi-kiu Lo, Nikola Ljubešić, Christof Monz, Makoto Morishita, Masaaki Nagata, Toshiaki Nakazawa, Santanu Pal, Matt Post, and Marcos Zampieri. 2020. Findings of the 2020 conference on machine translation (WMT20). In *Proceedings of the Fifth Conference on Machine Translation*, pages 1–55, Online. Association for Computational Linguistics.

Loïc Barrault, Ondřej Bojar, Marta R. Costa-jussà, Christian Federmann, Mark Fishel, Yvette Graham, Barry Haddow, Matthias Huck, Philipp Koehn, Shervin Malmasi, Christof Monz, Mathias Müller, Santanu Pal, Matt Post, and Marcos Zampieri. 2019. Findings of the 2019 conference on machine translation (WMT19). In *Proceedings of the Fourth Conference on Machine Translation (Volume 2: Shared Task Papers, Day 1)*, pages 1–61, Florence, Italy. Association for Computational Linguistics.

Emanuele Bastianelli, Andrea Vanzo, Pawel Swietojanski, and Verena Rieser. 2020. SLURP: A spoken language understanding resource package. In *Proceedings of the 2020 Conference on Empirical Methods in Natural Language Processing (EMNLP)*, pages 7252–7262, Online. Association for Computational Linguistics.

Ondřej Bojar, Christian Buck, Christian Federmann, Barry Haddow, Philipp Koehn, Johannes Leveling, Christof Monz, Pavel Pecina, Matt Post, Herve Saint-Amand, Radu Soricut, Lucia Specia, and Aleš Tamchyna. 2014. Findings of the 2014 workshop on statistical machine translation. In *Proceedings of the Ninth Workshop on Statistical Machine Translation*, pages 12–58, Baltimore, Maryland, USA. Association for Computational Linguistics.

Samuel Cahyawijaya, Genta Indra Winata, Bryan Wilie, Karissa Vincentio, Xiaohong Li, Adhiguna Kuncoro, Sebastian Ruder, Zhi Yuan Lim, Syafri Bahar, Masayu Khodra, Ayu Purwarianti, and Pascale Fung. 2021. IndoNLG: Benchmark and resources for evaluating Indonesian natural language generation. In *Proceedings of the 2021 Conference on Empirical Methods in Natural Language Processing*, pages 8875–8898, Online and Punta Cana, Dominican Republic. Association for Computational Linguistics.

Alexis Conneau, Kartikay Khandelwal, Naman Goyal, Vishrav Chaudhary, Guillaume Wenzek, Francisco Guzmán, Edouard Grave, Myle Ott, Luke Zettlemoyer, and Veselin Stoyanov. 2020. Unsupervised cross-lingual representation learning at scale. In *Proceedings of the 58th Annual Meeting of the Association for Computational Linguistics*, pages 8440–8451, Online. Association for Computational Linguistics.

Raj Dabre, Chenhui Chu, and Anoop Kunchukuttan. 2020. A survey of multilingual neural machine translation. *ACM Comput. Surv.*, 53(5).

Raj Dabre, Atsushi Fujita, and Chenhui Chu. 2019. Exploiting multilingualism through multistage finetuning for low-resource neural machine translation.

In *Proceedings of the 2019 Conference on Empirical Methods in Natural Language Processing and the 9th International Joint Conference on Natural Language Processing (EMNLP-IJCNLP)*, pages 1410–1416, Hong Kong, China. Association for Computational Linguistics.

Raj Dabre, Himani Shrotriya, Anoop Kunchukuttan, Ratish Puduppully, Mitesh Khapra, and Pratyush Kumar. 2022. IndicBART: A pre-trained model for indic natural language generation. In *Findings of the Association for Computational Linguistics: ACL 2022*, pages 1849–1863, Dublin, Ireland. Association for Computational Linguistics.

Sumanth Doddapaneni, Rahul Aralikatte, Gowtham Ramesh, Shreya Goyal, Mitesh M. Khapra, Anoop Kunchukuttan, and Pratyush Kumar. 2023. Towards leaving no indic language behind: Building monolingual corpora, benchmark and models for indic languages.

Ahmed El-Kishky, Vishrav Chaudhary, Francisco Guzmán, and Philipp Koehn. 2020. CCAligned: A massive collection of cross-lingual web-document pairs. In *Proceedings of the 2020 Conference on Empirical Methods in Natural Language Processing (EMNLP)*, pages 5960–5969, Online. Association for Computational Linguistics.

Angela Fan, Shruti Bhosale, Holger Schwenk, Zhiyi Ma, Ahmed El-Kishky, Siddharth Goyal, Mandeep Baines, Onur Celebi, Guillaume Wenzek, Vishrav Chaudhary, Naman Goyal, Tom Birch, Vitaliy Liptchinsky, Sergey Edunov, Edouard Grave, Michael Auli, and Armand Joulin. 2020. Beyond english-centric multilingual machine translation.

Christian Federmann, Tom Kocmi, and Ying Xin. 2022. NTREX-128 – news test references for MT evaluation of 128 languages. In *Proceedings of the First Workshop on Scaling Up Multilingual Evaluation*, pages 21–24, Online. Association for Computational Linguistics.

William Fedus, Barret Zoph, and Noam Shazeer. 2022. Switch transformers: Scaling to trillion parameter models with simple and efficient sparsity. *The Journal of Machine Learning Research*, 23(1):5232–5270.

Jack FitzGerald, Christopher Hench, Charith Peris, Scott Mackie, Kay Rottmann, Ana Sanchez, Aaron Nash, Liam Urbach, Vishesh Kakarala, Richa Singh, Swetha Ranganath, Laurie Crist, Misha Britan, Wouter Leeuwis, Gokhan Tur, and Prem Natarajan. 2022. Massive: A 1m-example multilingual natural language understanding dataset with 51 typologically-diverse languages. *arXiv preprint arXiv: Arxiv-2204.08582*.

Naman Goyal, Cynthia Gao, Vishrav Chaudhary, Peng-Jen Chen, Guillaume Wenzek, Da Ju, Sanjana Krishnan, Marc'Aurelio Ranzato, Francisco Guzmán, and Angela Fan. 2022. The Flores-101 evaluation benchmark for low-resource and multilingual machine translation. *Transactions of the Association for Computational Linguistics*, 10:522–538.

Sepp Hochreiter and Jürgen Schmidhuber. 1997. Long short-term memory. *Neural computation*, 9(8):1735–1780.

Girish Nath Jha. 2010. The TDIL program and the Indian langauge corpora intitiative (ILCI). In *Proceedings of the Seventh International Conference on Language Resources and Evaluation (LREC'10)*, Valletta, Malta. European Language Resources Association (ELRA).

Melvin Johnson, Mike Schuster, Quoc V. Le, Maxim Krikun, Yonghui Wu, Zhifeng Chen, Nikhil Thorat, Fernanda Viégas, Martin Wattenberg, Greg Corrado, Macduff Hughes, and Jeffrey Dean. 2017. Google's multilingual neural machine translation system: Enabling zero-shot translation. *Transactions of the Association for Computational Linguistics*, 5:339–351.

Divyanshu Kakwani, Anoop Kunchukuttan, Satish Golla, Gokul N.C., Avik Bhattacharyya, Mitesh M. Khapra, and Pratyush Kumar. 2020. IndicNLPSuite: Monolingual corpora, evaluation benchmarks and pre-trained multilingual language models for Indian languages. In *Findings of the Association for Computational Linguistics: EMNLP 2020*, pages 4948–4961, Online. Association for Computational Linguistics.

Tom Kocmi, Christian Federmann, Roman Grundkiewicz, Marcin Junczys-Dowmunt, Hitokazu Matsushita, and Arul Menezes. 2021. To ship or not to ship: An extensive evaluation of automatic metrics for machine translation. In *Proceedings of the Sixth Conference on Machine Translation*, pages 478–494, Online. Association for Computational Linguistics.

Xiang Kong, Adithya Renduchintala, James Cross, Yuqing Tang, Jiatao Gu, and Xian Li. 2021. Multilingual neural machine translation with deep encoder and multiple shallow decoders. In *Proceedings of the 16th Conference of the European Chapter of the Association for Computational Linguistics: Main Volume*, pages 1613–1624, Online. Association for Computational Linguistics.

Fajri Koto, Afshin Rahimi, Jey Han Lau, and Timothy Baldwin. 2020. IndoLEM and IndoBERT: A benchmark dataset and pre-trained language model for Indonesian NLP. In *Proceedings of the 28th International Conference on Computational Linguistics*, pages 757–770, Barcelona, Spain (Online). International Committee on Computational Linguistics.

Taku Kudo and John Richardson. 2018. SentencePiece: A simple and language independent subword tokenizer and detokenizer for neural text processing. In *Proceedings of the 2018 Conference on Empirical Methods in Natural Language Processing: System Demonstrations*, pages 66–71, Brussels, Belgium. Association for Computational Linguistics.

Anoop Kunchukuttan. 2020. The IndicNLP Library. https://github.com/anoopkunchukuttan/indic_nlp_library/blob/master/docs/indicnlp.pdf.

Anoop Kunchukuttan and Pushpak Bhattacharyya. 2020. Utilizing language relatedness to improve machine translation: A case study on languages of the indian subcontinent.

Zuchao Li, Yiran Wang, Masao Utiyama, Eiichiro Sumita, Hai Zhao, and Taro Watanabe. 2022. What works and doesn't work, a deep decoder for neural machine translation. In *Findings of the Association for Computational Linguistics: ACL 2022*, pages 459–471, Dublin, Ireland. Association for Computational Linguistics.

Daniel Licht, Cynthia Gao, Janice Lam, Francisco Guzmán, Mona T. Diab, and Philipp Koehn. 2022. Consistent human evaluation of machine translation across language pairs. In *Conference of the Association for Machine Translation in the Americas*.

Nikita Moghe, Tom Sherborne, Mark Steedman, and Alexandra Birch. 2022. Extrinsic evaluation of machine translation metrics.

Tasnim Mohiuddin, Philipp Koehn, Vishrav Chaudhary, James Cross, Shruti Bhosale, and Shafiq Joty. 2022. Data selection curriculum for neural machine translation. In *Findings of the Association for Computational Linguistics: EMNLP 2022*, pages 1569–1582, Abu Dhabi, United Arab Emirates. Association for Computational Linguistics.

Toshiaki Nakazawa, Hideki Nakayama, Chenchen Ding, Raj Dabre, Shohei Higashiyama, Hideya Mino, Isao Goto, Win Pa Pa, Anoop Kunchukuttan, Shantipriya Parida, Ondřej Bojar, Chenhui Chu, Akiko Eriguchi, Kaori Abe, Yusuke Oda, and Sadao Kurohashi. 2021. Overview of the 8th workshop on Asian translation. In *Proceedings of the 8th Workshop on Asian Translation (WAT2021)*, pages 1–45, Online. Association for Computational Linguistics.

Toshiaki Nakazawa, Hideki Nakayama, Chenchen Ding, Raj Dabre, Shohei Higashiyama, Hideya Mino, Isao Goto, Win Pa Pa, Anoop Kunchukuttan, Shantipriya Parida, Ondřej Bojar, and Sadao Kurohashi. 2020. Overview of the 7th workshop on Asian translation. In *Proceedings of the 7th Workshop on Asian Translation*, pages 1–44, Suzhou, China. Association for Computational Linguistics.

Kishore Papineni, Salim Roukos, Todd Ward, and Wei-Jing Zhu. 2002. Bleu: a method for automatic evaluation of machine translation. In *Proceedings of the 40th Annual Meeting of the Association for Computational Linguistics*, pages 311–318, Philadelphia, Pennsylvania, USA. Association for Computational Linguistics.

Maja Popović. 2015. chrF: character n-gram F-score for automatic MT evaluation. In *Proceedings of the Tenth Workshop on Statistical Machine Translation*, pages 392–395, Lisbon, Portugal. Association for Computational Linguistics.

Maja Popović. 2017. chrF++: words helping character n-grams. In *Proceedings of the Second Conference on Machine Translation*, pages 612–618, Copenhagen, Denmark. Association for Computational Linguistics.

Matt Post. 2018. A call for clarity in reporting BLEU scores. In *Proceedings of the Third Conference on Machine Translation: Research Papers*, pages 186–191, Brussels, Belgium. Association for Computational Linguistics.

Gowtham Ramesh, Sumanth Doddapaneni, Aravinth Bheemaraj, Mayank Jobanputra, Raghavan AK, Ajitesh Sharma, Sujit Sahoo, Harshita Diddee, Mahalakshmi J, Divyanshu Kakwani, Navneet Kumar, Aswin Pradeep, Srihari Nagaraj, Kumar Deepak, Vivek Raghavan, Anoop Kunchukuttan, Pratyush Kumar, and Mitesh Shantadevi Khapra. 2022. Samanantar: The largest publicly available parallel corpora collection for 11 Indic languages. *Transactions of the Association for Computational Linguistics*, 10:145–162.

Ricardo Rei, José G. C. de Souza, Duarte Alves, Chrysoula Zerva, Ana C Farinha, Taisiya Glushkova, Alon Lavie, Luisa Coheur, and André F. T. Martins. 2022. COMET-22: Unbabel-IST 2022 submission for the metrics shared task. In *Proceedings of the Seventh Conference on Machine Translation (WMT)*, pages 578–585, Abu Dhabi, United Arab Emirates (Hybrid). Association for Computational Linguistics.

Ricardo Rei, Craig Stewart, Ana C Farinha, and Alon Lavie. 2020. COMET: A neural framework for MT evaluation. In *Proceedings of the 2020 Conference on Empirical Methods in Natural Language Processing (EMNLP)*, pages 2685–2702, Online. Association for Computational Linguistics.

Machel Reid, Junjie Hu, Graham Neubig, and Yutaka Matsuo. 2021. AfroMT: Pretraining strategies and reproducible benchmarks for translation of 8 African languages. In *Proceedings of the 2021 Conference on Empirical Methods in Natural Language Processing*, pages 1306–1320, Online and Punta Cana, Dominican Republic. Association for Computational Linguistics.

D.E. Rumelhart, G.E. Hintont, and R.J. Williams. 1986. Learning representations by back-propagating errors. *Nature*, 323(6088):533–536.

Holger Schwenk, Guillaume Wenzek, Sergey Edunov, Edouard Grave, Armand Joulin, and Angela Fan. 2021. CCMatrix: Mining billions of high-quality parallel sentences on the web. In *Proceedings of the 59th Annual Meeting of the Association for Computational Linguistics and the 11th International Joint*

*Conference on Natural Language Processing (Volume 1: Long Papers)*, pages 6490–6500, Online. Association for Computational Linguistics.

Rico Sennrich, Barry Haddow, and Alexandra Birch. 2016. Neural machine translation of rare words with subword units. In *Proceedings of the 54th Annual Meeting of the Association for Computational Linguistics (Volume 1: Long Papers)*, pages 1715–1725, Berlin, Germany. Association for Computational Linguistics.

Ilya Sutskever, Oriol Vinyals, and Quoc V Le. 2014. Sequence to sequence learning with neural networks. In *Advances in Neural Information Processing Systems*, volume 27. Curran Associates, Inc.

NLLB Team, Marta R. Costa-jussà, James Cross, Onur Çelebi, Maha Elbayad, Kenneth Heafield, Kevin Heffernan, Elahe Kalbassi, Janice Lam, Daniel Licht, Jean Maillard, Anna Sun, Skyler Wang, Guillaume Wenzek, Al Youngblood, Bapi Akula, Loic Barrault, Gabriel Mejia Gonzalez, Prangthip Hansanti, John Hoffman, Semarley Jarrett, Kaushik Ram Sadagopan, Dirk Rowe, Shannon Spruit, Chau Tran, Pierre Andrews, Necip Fazil Ayan, Shruti Bhosale, Sergey Edunov, Angela Fan, Cynthia Gao, Vedanuj Goswami, Francisco Guzmán, Philipp Koehn, Alexandre Mourachko, Christophe Ropers, Safiyyah Saleem, Holger Schwenk, and Jeff Wang. 2022. No language left behind: Scaling human-centered machine translation.

Ashish Vaswani, Noam Shazeer, Niki Parmar, Jakob Uszkoreit, Llion Jones, Aidan N. Gomez, Lukasz Kaiser, and Illia Polosukhin. 2017. Attention is all you need. In *Advances in Neural Information Processing Systems 30: Annual Conference on Neural Information Processing Systems 2017, December 4-9, 2017, Long Beach, CA, USA*, pages 5998–6008.

David Vilar, Markus Freitag, Colin Cherry, Jiaming Luo, Viresh Ratnakar, and George Foster. 2022. Prompting palm for translation: Assessing strategies and performance. *arXiv preprint arXiv: 2211.09102*.

BigScience Workshop, :, Teven Le Scao, Angela Fan, Christopher Akiki, Ellie Pavlick, Suzana Ilić, Daniel Hesslow, Roman Castagné, Alexandra Sasha Luccioni, François Yvon, Matthias Gallé, Jonathan Tow, Alexander M. Rush, Stella Biderman, Albert Webson, Pawan Sasanka Ammanamanchi, Thomas Wang, Benoît Sagot, Niklas Muennighoff, Albert Villanova del Moral, Olatunji Ruwase, Rachel Bawden, Stas Bekman, Angelina McMillan-Major, Iz Beltagy, Huu Nguyen, Lucile Saulnier, Samson Tan, Pedro Ortiz Suarez, Victor Sanh, Hugo Laurençon, Yacine Jernite, Julien Launay, Margaret Mitchell, Colin Raffel, Aaron Gokaslan, Adi Simhi, Aitor Soroa, Alham Fikri Aji, Amit Alfassy, Anna Rogers, Ariel Kreisberg Nitzav, Canwen Xu, Chenghao Mou, Chris Emezue, Christopher Klamm, Colin Leong, Daniel van Strien, David Ifeoluwa Adelani, Dragomir Radev, Eduardo González Ponferrada, Efrat Levkovizh, Ethan Kim, Eyal Bar Natan, Francesco De Toni, Gérard Dupont, Germán Kruszewski, Giada Pistilli, Hady Elsahar, Hamza Benyamina, Hieu Tran, Ian Yu, Idris Abdulmumin, Isaac Johnson, Itziar Gonzalez-Dios, Javier de la Rosa, Jenny Chim, Jesse Dodge, Jian Zhu, Jonathan Chang, Jörg Frohberg, Joseph Tobing, Joydeep Bhattacharjee, Khalid Almubarak, Kimbo Chen, Kyle Lo, Leandro Von Werra, Leon Weber, Long Phan, Loubna Ben allal, Ludovic Tanguy, Manan Dey, Manuel Romero Muñoz, Maraim Masoud, María Grandury, Mario Šaško, Max Huang, Maximin Coavoux, Mayank Singh, Mike Tian-Jian Jiang, Minh Chien Vu, Mohammad A. Jauhar, Mustafa Ghaleb, Nishant Subramani, Nora Kassner, Nurulaqilla Khamis, Olivier Nguyen, Omar Espejel, Ona de Gibert, Paulo Villegas, Peter Henderson, Pierre Colombo, Priscilla Amuok, Quentin Lhoest, Rheza Harliman, Rishi Bommasani, Roberto Luis López, Rui Ribeiro, Salomey Osei, Sampo Pyysalo, Sebastian Nagel, Shamik Bose, Shamsuddeen Hassan Muhammad, Shanya Sharma, Shayne Longpre, Somaieh Nikpoor, Stanislav Silberberg, Suhas Pai, Sydney Zink, Tiago Timponi Torrent, Timo Schick, Tristan Thrush, Valentin Danchev, Vassilina Nikoulina, Veronika Laippala, Violette Lepercq, Vrinda Prabhu, Zaid Alyafeai, Zeerak Talat, Arun Raja, Benjamin Heinzerling, Chenglei Si, Davut Emre Taşar, Elizabeth Salesky, Sabrina J. Mielke, Wilson Y. Lee, Abheesht Sharma, Andrea Santilli, Antoine Chaffin, Arnaud Stiegler, Debajyoti Datta, Eliza Szczechla, Gunjan Chhablani, Han Wang, Harshit Pandey, Hendrik Strobelt, Jason Alan Fries, Jos Rozen, Leo Gao, Lintang Sutawika, M Saiful Bari, Maged S. Al-shaibani, Matteo Manica, Nihal Nayak, Ryan Teehan, Samuel Albanie, Sheng Shen, Srulik Ben-David, Stephen H. Bach, Taewoon Kim, Tali Bers, Thibault Fevry, Trishala Neeraj, Urmish Thakker, Vikas Raunak, Xiangru Tang, Zheng-Xin Yong, Zhiqing Sun, Shaked Brody, Yallow Uri, Hadar Tojarieh, Adam Roberts, Hyung Won Chung, Jaesung Tae, Jason Phang, Ofir Press, Conglong Li, Deepak Narayanan, Hatim Bourfoune, Jared Casper, Jeff Rasley, Max Ryabinin, Mayank Mishra, Minjia Zhang, Mohammad Shoeybi, Myriam Peyrounette, Nicolas Patry, Nouamane Tazi, Omar Sanseviero, Patrick von Platen, Pierre Cornette, Pierre François Lavallée, Rémi Lacroix, Samyam Rajbhandari, Sanchit Gandhi, Shaden Smith, Stéphane Requena, Suraj Patil, Tim Dettmers, Ahmed Baruwa, Amanpreet Singh, Anastasia Cheveleva, Anne-Laure Ligozat, Arjun Subramonian, Aurélie Névéol, Charles Lovering, Dan Garrette, Deepak Tunuguntla, Ehud Reiter, Ekaterina Taktasheva, Ekaterina Voloshina, Eli Bogdanov, Genta Indra Winata, Hailey Schoelkopf, Jan-Christoph Kalo, Jekaterina Novikova, Jessica Zosa Forde, Jordan Clive, Jungo Kasai, Ken Kawamura, Liam Hazan, Marine Carpuat, Miruna Clinciu, Najoung Kim, Newton Cheng, Oleg Serikov, Omer Antverg, Oskar van der Wal, Rui Zhang, Ruochen Zhang, Sebastian Gehrmann, Shachar Mirkin, Shani Pais, Tatiana Shavrina, Thomas Scialom, Tian Yun, Tomasz Limisiewicz, Verena Rieser, Vitaly Protasov, Vladislav Mikhailov, Yada Pruksachatkun, Yonatan Belinkov, Zachary Bamberger, Zdeněk Kasner, Alice Rueda, Amanda Pestana, Amir Feizpour, Ammar Khan, Amy Faranak, Ana Santos, Anthony Hevia, Antigona Unldreaj, Arash Aghagol, Arezoo Abdollahi, Aycha Tammour, Azadeh HajiHosseini, Bahareh Behroozi, Benjamin Ajibade, Bharat Saxena, Carlos Muñoz Ferrandis, Danish Contractor, David Lansky, Davis David, Douwe Kiela, Duong A. Nguyen, Edward Tan, Emi Baylor, Ezinwanne Ozoani, Fatima Mirza, Frankline Ononiwu, Habib Rezanejad, Hessie Jones, Indrani Bhattacharya, Irene Solaiman, Irina Sedenko, Isar Nejadgholi, Jesse Passmore, Josh Seltzer, Julio Bonis Sanz, Livia Dutra, Mairon Samagaio, Maraim Elbadri, Margot Mieskes, Marissa Gerchick, Martha Akinlolu, Michael McKenna, Mike Qiu, Muhammed Ghauri, Mykola Burynok, Nafis Abrar, Nazneen Rajani, Nour Elkott, Nour Fahmy, Olanrewaju Samuel, Ran An, Rasmus Kromann, Ryan Hao, Samira Alizadeh, Sarmad Shubber, Silas Wang, Sourav Roy, Sylvain Viguier, Thanh Le, Tobi Oyebade, Trieu Le, Yoyo Yang, Zach Nguyen, Abhinav Ramesh Kashyap, Alfredo Palasciano, Alison Callahan, Anima Shukla, Antonio Miranda-Escalada, Ayush Singh, Benjamin Beilharz, Bo Wang, Caio Brito, Chenxi Zhou, Chirag Jain, Chuxin Xu, Clémentine Fourrier, Daniel León Periñán, Daniel Molano, Dian Yu, Enrique Manjavacas, Fabio Barth, Florian Fuhrimann, Gabriel Altay, Giyaseddin Bayrak, Gully Burns, Helena U. Vrabec, Imane Bello, Ishani Dash, Jihyun Kang, John Giorgi, Jonas Golde, Jose David Posada, Karthik Rangasai Sivaraman, Lokesh Bulchandani, Lu Liu, Luisa Shinzato, Madeleine Hahn de Bykhovetz, Maiko Takeuchi, Marc Pàmies, Maria A Castillo, Marianna Nezhurina, Mario Sänger, Matthias Samwald, Michael Cullan, Michael Weinberg, Michiel De Wolf, Mina Mihaljcic, Minna Liu, Moritz Freidank, Myungsun Kang, Natasha Seelam, Nathan Dahlberg, Nicholas Michio Broad, Nikolaus Muellner, Pascale Fung, Patrick Haller, Ramya Chandrasekhar, Renata Eisenberg, Robert Martin, Rodrigo Canalli, Rosaline Su, Ruisi Su, Samuel Cahyawijaya, Samuele Garda, Shlok S Deshmukh, Shubhanshu Mishra, Sid Kiblawi, Simon Ott, Sinee Sang-aroonsiri, Srishti Kumar, Stefan Schweter, Sushil Bharati, Tanmay Laud, Théo Gigant, Tomoya Kainuma, Wojciech Kusa, Yanis Labrak, Yash Shailesh Bajaj, Yash Venkatraman, Yifan Xu, Yingxin Xu, Yu Xu, Zhe Tan, Zhongli Xie, Zifan Ye, Mathilde Bras, Younes Belkada, and Thomas Wolf. 2023. Bloom: A 176b-parameter open-access multilingual language model.

Linting Xue, Noah Constant, Adam Roberts, Mihir Kale, Rami Al-Rfou, Aditya Siddhant, Aditya Barua, and Colin Raffel. 2021. mT5: A massively multilingual pre-trained text-to-text transformer. In *Proceedings of the 2021 Conference of the North American Chapter of the Association for Computational Linguistics: Human Language Technologies*, pages 483–498, Online. Association for Computational Linguistics.

Mike Zhang and Antonio Toral. 2019. The effect of translationese in machine translation test sets. In *Proceedings of the Fourth Conference on Machine Translation (Volume 1: Research Papers)*, pages 73–81, Florence, Italy. Association for Computational Linguistics.